The Presbyterian
Way of Life

Also by the author

Christianity on the Frontier

God's Order

Preface to Christian Theology

The Other Spanish Christ

The
PRESBYTERIAN
Way of Life

✤ *by* ✤

JOHN A. MACKAY

PRENTICE-HALL, INC.

Englewood Cliffs, N. J.

Library of Congress Catalog Card Number 60-14198

Printed in the United States of America

69730-T

ISBN: 978-1-4391-9403-4

*To all who down the years have helped me under-
stand my Presbyterian heritage and in its spirit have
inspired me to seek the unity of the one Faith, for
the mission of the one Church, through obedience to
the one Lord, this book is dedicated.*

Contents

Prologue

THE writing of this book has stirred both memory and reflection. Memory has carried the author back across the years along the road it has been his lot to travel as a Presbyterian Christian.

A Presbyterian Pilgrim

In the providence of God I have had occasion to run the whole gamut of Presbyterianism. Until I was twenty-four years of age, I belonged to a small denomination in the Highlands of Scotland which claims, and glories in the claim that it embodies the quintessence of the Reformed faith, that is, the great Calvinistic tradition to which Presbyterianism belongs. Exulting in the orthodoxy of its beliefs and the purity of its worship, this minute and diminishing community of faith continues to maintain a disdainful aloofness from all other church bodies, Presbyterian and non-Presbyterian alike. Deep, however, in the spirit of its members is an eschatological hope. This hope was expressed to me in my early teens by one of the denomination's saintly laymen. "The other churches may despise us today," said this Scottish Highlander, "but when the Millennium comes, they will all rally to the banner of truth which God has given to our Church."

Despite the distance I have moved from this sentiment of old Richard Cameron, I cannot recall my boyhood days without the words of that sacred song which an exiled Hebrew wrote by the "waters of Babylon," coming to my lips in melody, "If I forget thee, oh Jerusalem, let my tongue cleave to the roof of my mouth." For it was in the fellowship of this rigid and diminutive church community, that God first spoke to me, that the Bible became an exciting book to me, that Jesus Christ became dear to me, that that Christian discipleship became real to me.

It was under the auspices of another Presbyterian denomination in Scotland that I discovered the Hispanic world, and became the first Presbyterian missionary to Peru. To this denomination, I owe a very deep debt of gratitude. I cherish its name and the memory of days bye-gone, but its present sectarian trend, so alien to its tradition, has brought me untold sorrow.

As past president of the World Presbyterian Alliance, as a minister for nearly thirty years of Presbyterianism's leading denomination, and the President for more than twenty of its oldest and largest theological seminary, I have, in God's providence, been given an unusual opportunity to know the very diversified confessional family to which I belong. I have had occasion to experience Presbyterianism in both its sectarian and its ecumenical forms.

The work involved in preparing the present volume has been a thrilling and soul-searching experience. It has made it possible for me to survey in leisurely fashion the history and the structure, the ideas and the attitudes, of Presbyterian churches, in order to interpret the significance of Presbyterianism within the context of our time and the life of the Church Universal. In describing the "Presbyterian Way," and assessing its contribution to Christianity and the world, I have been obliged also to consider this contribution in relation to my own spiritual development and outlook, and to the total task of the Christian Church today.

In so doing I have become keenly aware that my life is the embodiment of a paradox. The same paradox, however, marks the life of many another Christian in our time. On the one hand, I am today a more convinced and loyal Presbyterian than I have ever been before. On the other hand, I am less of a Presbyterian absolutist and sectarian than at any time in my life. Never did I thank God so much as I now do for my Presbyterian heritage of faith and life and for the present witness of my denomination. Yet never have I been so grateful to the Almighty for the heritage and witness of other Christian churches and traditions. To many of these I have owed an incalculable debt in the years of my pilgrimage. For to them too the Holy Spirit has given much, and through them He has done much that is needed today in the life and witness of the Holy Catholic Church.

ON THE ECUMENICAL ROAD

Speaking therefore as a Presbyterian, let me tell of what I owe to other Christians. In my early youth, books by Baptists, especially John Bunyan and Charles Haddon Spurgeon, made a lasting impression upon me. As a university student in Aberdeen, I attended a Baptist church, there being no church of my own denomination in the city. It was in a Baptist mission hall that I made my first public presentation of the Christian Gospel. I married a Baptist bride.

While engaged in graduate study in Madrid, Spain, preparatory to ordination and my commissioning as a missionary to Latin America, I frequently attended a meeting place where services were conducted by Plymouth Brethren from England. The first time I ventured to speak in public in the Spanish tongue was at a cottage meeting conducted in a workmen's suburb of Madrid, to which I had been invited by the Brethren pastor.

It was in those days that I made my first acquaintance with the great Spanish mystics of the sixteenth century whom, I was soon to discover, Spanish Protestants claim as their own. I was introduced to Saint John of the Cross, to Saint Theresa of Avila, to Augustinian Friar, Luis de Leon, and to Luis de Granada, of the order of St. Dominic. The writings of these sixteenth century Catholic authors, some of which were penned in prisons of the Inquisition, opened up to me unsuspected evangelical vistas and a forgotten Christo-centric heritage in the Hispanic religious tradition.

What have I not owed down the years since then to the inspiration of the lyrical poetry of Luis de Leon and to his theological masterpiece *The Names of Christ* which he wrote during a four year's imprisonment in the Castilian city of Valledolid! What can repay my debt to the *Ascent of Mount Carmel*, the matchless mystic poem of John of the Cross, which was penned in an Inquisition prison cell in Toledo.

When, as sometimes happens, I am accused of being an anti-Catholic bigot, I can truthfully say this as an ardent Protestant and a loyal Presbyterian: If I have a saint, it is that great Christian soul Theresa of Avila, author of *The Dwelling Places* (Las Moradas) and of an autobiography *Libro de Mi Vida*, which is one of the few peers in literature of St. Augustine's *Confessions*.

I have had many occasions during my life to bear witness by lip and pen to my indebtedness to that great Spaniard, Miguel de Unamuno. It was he, the successor of Luis de Leon in the University of Salamanca, the man whom the church of his fathers excommunicated in 1914, and whose works it subsequently placed on the Index, who opened up to me the spiritual riches of the Spanish Mystics and Reformers.

In the course of sixteen years spent in Latin America, I enjoyed priceless opportunities for intimate Christian fellowship outside my immediate Presbyterian relationship. I felt the inspiration of "Faith missionaries." I experienced the thrill of the Pentecostal movement which swept Chilean society. I rejoiced in the unique spiritual role of a non-ecclesiastical organization like the Young Men's Christian Association which I served for seven years, when it takes seriously the term "Christian." In Uruguay I discovered the soul of Methodism. While residing in Montevideo, my family and I, in the absence of a Presbyterian congregation, became related to a Methodist Episcopal church.

It was in the late twenties and early thirties of the century, while I roved the Latin-American world endeavoring to interpret Christ and Christianity in the university centers, that I discovered the Lutheran, Soren Kierkegaard. During those same years I became acquainted with the writings of that son of Russian Orthodoxy, Feodor Dostoevski. Both of these writers opened up for me new insights into the human and the Divine, into Christ and the Church.

In more recent years, many abiding friendships have been formed across confessional boundaries. Meetings have been attended and work has been undertaken within the nascent Ecumenical Movement to which my denomination, inspired by the thought and spirit of John Calvin, has been consistently committed.

TOWARD THE CITY OF GOD

Yet, notwithstanding these experiences, my grateful spirit has not been de-Presbyterianized. I believe with greater fervor, and I trust, for more intelligent reasons than ever before in my life, that there are some unique elements in Presbyterianism. To these elements that belong to the essence of the one Church, which is Christ's Body, reference will be made in due course.

On the other hand this, too, has happened. It has become clear to me that there are other Christian churches which have in their tradition and witness elements which equally belong to the essence of Christ's Church.

The Holy Spirit has not yet revealed the organizational

structure which is fitted to express the order and to channel
the life of the Holy Catholic Church on the road of history.
The true form of the One Church will become manifest only
when all the churches rededicate themselves afresh to Jesus
Christ the sole Head of the Church and when, in loyal obedience to Him, they accept their missionary calling. For only
when the churches fulfill the mission of Christ can they give
creative, visible expression of their unity in Christ.

I have this dual conviction. Because Jesus Christ is Lord of
the Church and of history, there is no future to a proud absolutistic confessionalism. This is true whether it be the absolutism that is found in the small Presbyterian denomination in
which I was brought up, or the absolution which marks
Christianity's largest communion—the Roman Catholic
Church. I am equally convinced, and for the same reason,
that there is no future to any vague ecumenism whose goal is
the minimum common ground of Christian agreement.

Let me add this observation. The task to which Prentice-
Hall has called representatives of leading American denominations to interpret, each one, the confessional family to which
he belongs, is not unworthy of, but essential to the pursuit of
Christian unity in the Ecumenical Era. True unity can be
achieved only in one way. Each confession, after a process of
rigorous self-examination, carried on under the guidance of
the Holy Spirit, in the triple light of the Word of God, the history of the church and the challenge of the hour, must strip
itself of all accretions due to human pride and error. Let it
then, responsive to the imperious voice of Jesus Christ, seek
that unity which can be found only in mission.

May this book be a contribution to an understanding of the
"Presbyterian Way." In describing who Presbyterians are, and
where they have come from, and in interpreting the classical
core of Presbyterian belief and the pattern of Presbyterian life
and relationships, I will take the occasion to distill my reflections upon the genius of Presbyterianism and its unique place
in the church Universal. It is my deep desire that by the

perusal of these pages Presbyterians and others may be inspired and helped to tread the Christian road toward the City of God.

John A. Mackay

Chevy Chase
Maryland

PART ONE

The Presbyterian Understanding of Life

✠ 1 ✠

Presbyterianism
in the Perspective
of the Years

WHO PRESBYTERIANS ARE AND WHENCE THEY CAME

No time could be more propitious for a discussion of Presbyterianism. Reports of important anniversaries recently celebrated, with others still to come, have awakened lively interest in the question, "Who Are Presbyterians and where did they come from?"

During 1959, the Four Hundred Fiftieth Anniversary of the birth of a Christian churchman called John Calvin, whom Presbyterians hail as their spiritual father, was the occasion of great festivities. The same year the Reformed Church of France, which was organized through Calvin's influence, celebrated its Four Hundredth Anniversary. So too did the University of Geneva which Calvin founded.

These historic events bring vividly to memory the movement for Christian reform from which Presbyterianism stems, and

3

out of which came also the sister-Reformed churches of Europe and America. The present year marks the Four Hundredth Anniversary of the Scottish Reformation which took place under the leadership of Calvin's student and friend, John Knox. This celebration will be an impressive reminder of that religious revolution which is the source of the many Presbyterian Churches found today in Great Britain and the Americas, in Africa, Asia and Australia.

Still another anniversary is in prospect which will have great significance for the Reformed family of churches to which Presbyterian churches belong. In 1963 four hundred years will have passed since the publication of the famous *Heidelberg Catechism*. This marvelous compendium of Christian faith was originally published as the doctrinal standards of the Reformed Church in the Palatinate, which was the Rhineland State in the old German Empire. It is a known fact that this historic document profoundly influenced Presbyterianism in Scotland. What is also significant from an ecumenical point of view is that the *Heidelberg Catechism* constitutes a link with Lutheranism. It has been characterized by an eminent Scottish thinker of our time as "an exposition of Christian doctrine which brings together both Lutheran and Reformed teaching and as such has exercised a powerful mediating influence."

Yet, withal, to identify Presbyterians is not a simple task. It is probably easier to describe and classify the members of almost any of the main branches of the great Protestant family, with the possible exception of the Baptists, than it is to identify with any measure of adequacy and precision all those Christians who lay claim to the designation "Presbyterian."

The reasons for this are various. In a popular sense the term "Presbyterian" can be applied to all those churches in Continental Europe and in North America that bear the name "Reformed" in their official title. For all Presbyterians, as we shall see later, belong historically to the great "Reformed" family of churches whose immediate spiritual ancestors are the Reformers, Calvin and Zwingli. The majority of those churches are members of a world body whose official title is "The Alliance of the Reformed Churches Throughout the World Holding the Presbyterian Order." In English speaking countries this organization is popularly known as "The World Presbyterian Alliance."

But even when consideration is limited to those churches which explicitly call themselves "Presbyterian" a diversity still prevails. It is, of course, natural that churches should be distinguished from other churches by the name of the country in which they happen to be located. It is, therefore, not at all surprising that there should be "The Irish Presbyterian Church," "The Australian Presbyterian Church," "The Canadian Presbyterian Church," "The Korean Presbyterian Church," "The Brazilian Presbyterian Church" or "The Presbyterian Church in the U.S.A." Such distinctions, it is well to remember, are by no means peculiar to Presbyterianism. We are accustomed to speak of "The Church of Rome," "The Russian Orthodox Church," "The Greek Orthodox Church," "The Protestant Episcopal Church of North America," "The Church of South India."

Where the real confusion occurs is in the diversity of qualifying epithets which are found attached to many Presbyterian churches. These epithets are designed to express some historical witness or some theological position. There are some smaller denominations, for example, which append the terms "Free," "Reformed," "Bible," or "Orthodox," to the designation "Presbyterian" in their official title.

While all this is true and may be somewhat confusing to the uninitiated, several things need to be said. There is in Presbyterianism a "Way," a classical Christian tradition and a native genius which is peculiarly its own. It will be the aim of this study to explore and describe this "Presbyterian Way." In undertaking my present task, and while endeavoring to do justice to the witness and contribution of other Presbyterian Churches in the great central tradition, I shall have occasion to refer in a special manner and with greater frequency, although by no means exclusively, to Presbyterianism in the United States. Expected as I am to give particular attention to "The Presbyterian Way of Life" as it has manifested itself within the context of American religious history, this special emphasis is inevitable.

I have selected for special reference and as a main source of illustration, a particular member of the American Presbyterian family. This Church, the United Presbyterian Church in the U.S.A., is the largest denomination in the World Presbyterian household and is today the most influential. It also happens to be exceedingly representative in character, both as regards its historical development and its contemporary life. According to every criterion, it embodies the authentic genius of Presbyterianism as a manifestation of the Christian religion. In its history and life are found the concerns and the tensions, the perils and the failures, the victories and the visions that have marked the "Presbyterian Way." It is besides the church which I know best, the church of which I am a minister. It is the church, moreover, which, in full consistency with its Presbyterian heritage of faith, has made it possible for me to belong to and to serve Christ's Church Universal. For no one, let it be said emphatically, can be a Presbyterian if he is a mere Presbyterian.

Having said this, let me proceed to explore what it means to be Presbyterian, and to probe into the heritage of faith and life which is associated with that name.

It is important that we begin this study by taking a look at Presbyterian family connections.

CALVIN AND CALVINISTS

The forty-five million Presbyterians of the world scattered abroad in more than seventy countries are, with Lutherans and Anglicans, children of the Protestant Reformation of the Sixteenth Century. The spiritual father of Presbyterians was a Frenchman, John Calvin, who spent most of his life in the Swiss city of Geneva. At the age of twenty-seven, Calvin wrote a book called the *Institutes of the Christian Religion.* This book, which the author revised several times during his lifetime, became the main source of that interpretation of Christianity which is commonly designated "Reformed," and of that particular form of Church government by "Presbyters" or "elders," which is known as "Presbyterian." By his writings, lectures and public activities in the church and in the civil community in Geneva, Calvin became the principal figure in a religious reform movement which paralleled the great movement in Germany which is associated with the name of Martin Luther.

There is a memorial in Geneva known as the Reformation Monument, which is the symbol in art of the Calvinistic Reformation. It takes the form of a galaxy of immense statues. The figures of Calvin and the chief men associated with him in his reforming effort, Zwingli, Bucer, Farel, Beza and Knox, stand in horizontal array against a solid wall. This reform movement initiated by Calvin in the medieval church and society as an effort to restore the church to its pristine character lives on in the world of today in three different ways.

The Genevan Reform lives on *theologically* in that system of Christian doctrine known as Calvinism. It was Calvin who inspired and molded the religious thought of the non-Lutheran churches in Europe which call themselves "Reformed." He is also the theological father of that great group of Protestant denominations which are diversely known as Anglican, Congregationalist, Baptist and Presbyterian.

Ecclesiastically speaking, Calvinism created that form of church government in which the ultimate authority is vested in Presbytery. A Presbytery is a church court or judicatory composed of Presbyters, that is, ministers and laymen, in equal numbers, all of whom are democratically elected by the people.

Calvinism also left its imprint in *social* and *political institutions.* The principles for which Calvin and his colleagues stood were a potent factor in defeating the absolutist state in Europe and in creating democratic governments. Through the influence of Calvin's spiritual descendants, the Puritans of New England, Congregationalists, Baptists and Presbyterians, and of those other children located farther to the south, the Episcopalians and Presbyterians of New York and New Jersey, of Pennsylvania and Virginia, the basis of American democracy was laid and American freedom was won.

Taking farewell, however, for the time being of Presbyterianism's revered cousins and other family connections in the Calvinistic tradition, who bear quite diverse ecclesiastical names, let me now endeavor to answer with precision, who Presbyterians are and whence they came.

Let us turn, therefore, to the fountainhead of Presbyterianism, to that great reforming personality of the sixteenth century, John Calvin. Martin Luther, John Calvin and John Knox are enshrined in history's annals as the most dynamic and creative figures of the Protestant Reformation. Calvin stands at the head of the Reformed tradition, Luther at the head of the Lutheran tradition.

John Calvin, the father of Presbyterianism and of that religious orientation known as "Reformed," was one of the greatest men of his time and of all time. He was a very great scholar who has been appropriately called "The man of letters as saint." Calvin began his academic career as a student of the Greek and Latin classics and was a special devotee of Seneca the Stoic. He looked forward to law as his profession. But the young Humanist suddenly felt himself grasped by the Living God. This encounter completely changed the tenor of his life and the direction of his thoughts.

From that moment Calvin became a "God intoxicated man," in a sense more dynamically true than could be said even of the philosopher Spinoza. His humanistic studies, which he continued to love and cultivate, became the servant of a Christian commitment. His devotion to the thought of the great Stoics colored his attitude toward life so that, as one has stated, "Calvinism is Stoicism baptized into Christianity but renewed and exalted by the baptism." It is an interesting and symbolic fact, moreover, that the two men who gave Christianity its most dynamic interpretation in relation to the secular order in the sixteenth century, John Calvin, the Frenchman, and Ignatius of Loyola, the Spaniard, were educated about the same time, in the same university, and by the same teacher.

The profound religious experience, through which Calvin passed, of being grasped by a sovereign God, gave to all his subsequent thought an overmastering awareness of the transcendent majesty and sovereignty of the Almighty. Feeling himself to be thrust into a situation which he would not naturally have chosen, he developed a deep sense of mission. His great question became and continued to be "What does God want of me, of the Church, and of mankind?"

Regarding his momentous spiritual experience, Calvin spoke very little and never with that lyrical subjectivity which marks the life of Martin Luther. There is an emblem in religious art, however, called Calvin's Crest, which movingly describes his spirit and the nature of his devotion. In that crest is seen an outstretched arm; the hand grasps a heart in flame which it offers to Deity. These words encircle and interpret the symbols: "My heart I give Thee, Lord, eagerly and sincerely."

It can truly be said that Calvin the Humanist, the Stoic, the profound thinker, the matchless logician, became a theologian through his heart. This fact is extremely important for an adequate understanding of Presbyterianism. A system of religious thought and a form of church organization, which were created by a man whose heart was set on fire, cannot be true to their nature unless the reality of a life inflamed with a passion for God and accustomed to communion with God is given a central place. For deep in the heart of Calvinism, and in Presbyterianism in its truest and most classical form, resides a profound piety, that is, a personal experience of God linked to a passionate devotion to God. Piety thus understood provides light and direction for all Christian and humanistic learning. It is piety in this sense that provides the requisite dynamic for the conduct of church affairs and the application of Christianity to life in all its fullness. Piety has been the soul not only of classical Presbyterianism, but also of all genuine Christian witness, whatever be the Confessional family to which a Christian may belong.

Calvin's great book, *The Institutes of the Christian Religion,* was an effort to reach back to the Christianity of the Bible and the Apostolic Church. Taking the Scriptures alone, rather than Scripture and Tradition, as His supreme authority, and looking to the Holy Spirit rather than to the Church of his time for guidance, in his interpretation of the Christian truth, while being most deferential to the opinion of the great Fathers of the Church, Calvin sought to construct a system of Christian theology. In doing so he restored the Word of God, God's self-disclosure of Himself and His redemptive purpose in Holy Scripture as the supreme standard for life and doctrine. He was most sensitive, however, to tradition at its best. It was his desire to restore for the thought and life of his time the light and power of early Christianity that led him to make his *The Institutes of the Christian Religion* a commentary on the Apostles' Creed. In the whole realm of Christian thought only the famous *Summa Theologica* of the Roman Catholic monk and scholar, Thomas Aquinas, can be compared to Calvin's *Institutes* in sheer theological massiveness and in far-reaching influence. And interestingly enough, as recent studies have shown, there is much in common in the thought of these two great men.

Besides theology, Calvin wrote Commentaries on all the Books of the Bible, with the exception of the Book of Revelation. These Commentaries, because of the extraordinary insight and perspicacity which their author displays in expounding the Biblical text, continue to be consulted by contemporary scholars. The master commentator stopped short, however, at one point. He offered no interpretation of the Apocalypse. Unlike many of his successors, Presbyterians among them, Calvin found the closing book of the Bible far too difficult and mysterious for him to interpret in any authoritative way. He was assured regarding the direction in which history was going and of the certain triumph of Christ and his

Church. But he was too immersed in doing the will of God in the living present to be willing to take up his time in an armchair existence trying to blueprint the future.

The Genevan professor, when he grasped a Biblical truth, was not satisfied, as many professors have tended to be, with its merely academic formulation. He strove passionately to apply it to life in its wholeness, personal, social and political. In this respect Calvin differed from his great contemporary, Martin Luther. Luther abstained on principle from relating the sublime truths of the faith to the temporal order. Those two men held totally diverse views on the role of the Christian, and of the Christian Church, in relation to the world and its problems. Their difference of viewpoint in this regard was destined to become manifest in the subsequent history of the two great systems of thought and life which bear their names.

Calvin was convinced that both the Christian and the Christian Church should be concerned about, and participate in, the life of the world. In this regard he himself set the example. In Geneva he organized not only a church, but also a form of secular society in which God and the People, the principle of theocracy and the principle of democracy, were given their appropriate place. In due time the theological truths which Calvin proclaimed and the structure which he proposed for Church and State had their repercussions. New churches, democratic in their organization, soon came into being in various European lands. The influence of Calvin's ideas and social patterns soon became manifest in revolutionary movements in Great Britain and the Netherlands. "Calvin saved Europe," said Mark Pattison, the English man of letters. Had it not been for what has become known as Calvinism, the European continent would have been swept with totalitarian tyranny. It was not long before the children of Calvin, under diverse ecclesiastical names, founded the American Commonwealth, where a new conception of religious and political freedom was born.

Things happened too in the realms of international relations and economic thought. Grotius, a Calvinistic Dutchman, gave expression to the concept of International Law. Calvin's idea that it was legitimate for people to invest their money at interest, provided the amount of recompense asked was fair and equitable, gave birth to a new and creative form of business enterprise. Whatever opinions may be held regarding the nature and future of the capitalistic order and of what we know as Free Enterprise, this can be affirmed. Capitalism which was inspired by Calvin's ideas has produced creative results during a great historical epoch. Even should it eventually be succeeded by some other economic order, whatever that order may be, nothing can dim the luster of Capitalism's achievement nor the validity of the inspiration that gave it birth.

One further word regarding Calvin's influence. There is a sense in which the mainstream of the modern missionary movement had its immediate source in a fountain which God graciously opened in Geneva and which was fed from the Eternal Spring in Jerusalem. During his own lifetime and long before the Pilgrim Fathers, who were also his children, reached Plymouth Rock, John Calvin sent a Protestant missionary expedition to Brazil. Calvinist too was the Baptist, William Carey, who initiated the modern missionary movement in the English-speaking world; the Anglican, Henry Martyn, that brilliant young mathematician of the University of Cambridge who spent his brief but creative career in India; the Presbyterian, David Livingstone, missionary pioneer of Central Africa; and Robert Morrison, the Presbyterian who opened for the Gospel the age-long seclusion of China. A Calvinist also, and a Presbyterian, was Samuel Mills, one of a group of students of Williams College, Massachusetts, who once met for prayer beneath a haystack in a rain shower. Those students subsequently founded the American Board of Foreign Missions which was the first of the great foreign missionary societies in the United States.

SAINTHOOD IN THE SHADOW

But another note needs to be struck, a note of unspeakable sadness. John Calvin was a man subject to the limitations of finite and sinful human nature about which he wrote so extensively. He was also a child of his time, influenced by the atmosphere and the prejudices of the age in which he lived. His was a period in history when persecution for religious ideas regarded as heretical was passionately and conscientiously carried on. It was a time in which a religious tribunal known as the Inquisition sought to rid the world of dangerous heretics by sentencing them to death. Child of his generation, Calvin grievously erred. He committed the heinous sin of consenting to the execution, by burning, of a Spaniard named Servetus who had been convicted of heresy by a Genevan tribunal. The heretic was willing to call Jesus the "Son of the Eternal God" but he refused to call him "the Eternal Son of God."

It matters nothing that the Roman Catholic Church was also on the trail of Servetus, eager to bring him to the stake. Calvin's sin cannot be condoned or slurred over. He himself, in fact, would not want it to be forgotten. To the end of his days, he could not forgive himself for Servetus' death, any more than King David could for his act of adultery and murder, or St. Peter could for having cursed and denied his Lord.

There are people, unfortunately, whose knowledge of Calvin is willfully limited to his association with the Servetus affair. There are others whose estimate of him is darkened and prejudiced by this episode. For these, but especially for the sake of those who love Calvin's memory, who have been profoundly influenced by his ideas and have rejoiced in the transforming influence he has exercised in religion and civilization, let me be allowed to set this dismal event in its due perspective.

The man who more than any theologian diagnosed the reality of original sin in human nature became deeply aware of his own sin and was penitent for it. Calvin asked that when he died no monument should grace his tomb nor marking of any kind denote the place where his remains were laid. To this day no one knows where lies the dust of Geneva's greatest and most revered citizen. The only monument in Geneva erected to Calvin himself, apart from his stone statue in the great Reformation Monument, where he appears alongside other Protestant leaders, is the monument erected by the citizens of Geneva to the memory of Michael Servetus. In 1909, on the same spot where the Spanish heretic was burned, the most moving expiatory memorial in human history was unveiled. The unveiling took place during the celebration of the Four Hundredth Anniversary of Calvin's birth. Rendered into English the inscription on that memorial reads thus: "We, the respectful and grateful sons of Calvin, our Great Reformer, but condemning an error which was due to the age in which he lived, and being firmly devoted to liberty of conscience, according to the true principles of the Reformation and of the Gospel, have erected this expiatory monument."

Some comments are in order before we turn away our gaze for the present from the pioneer of the "Presbyterian Way."

First, the tragic event in Calvin's life to which allusion has just been made was not native to the spirit of the great Geneva Reformer. Neither was it representative of his Christian behavior. It was rather a doleful reprehensible aberration, totally out of harmony with the truth which he taught and the principles for which he stood. In this present age when churches and nations hitherto noted for their estrangement from one another are making efforts to establish fraternal relations, what would it not mean for the ecclesiastical and international climate, if hundreds, nay thousands of similar expiatory monuments were to be erected around the world! Presbyterians can take legitimate, if somber satisfaction, in the knowledge that the most famous of such expiatory monuments was inspired by the tradition to which they belong. Let them continue to walk in this "way."

A second comment falls to be made. The event that cast a dim shadow on a great career has been symbolical. The fanaticism, which momentarily seized the soul of John Calvin and his associates, has sometimes appeared in other forms in the course of Presbyterian history. There have been occasions in many lands when groups of Presbyterians felt so strongly about certain issues, whether in doctrine, in the church or society, that they developed a fanatical mania. In consequence Jesus Christ, His truth and His Church, were sometimes put to open shame. Gripped by this mood, some Presbyterians have glorified schism, absolutized trifles and non-essentials. By doing so they unwittingly betrayed the great principles for which John Calvin stood, and for which classical Presbyterianism, as I shall endeavor to describe it, continues to stand.

This said, we are ready to consider some of the main historical landmarks on the road which Reformed and Presbyterian pilgrims have traversed through the past four hundred years.

LANDMARKS ON THE PRESBYTERIAN WAY

While this is not a book on Presbyterian history, it is important for our understanding of the thought and life of Presbyterians today that we should take a retrospective look at some of the main episodes in the development of the Presbyterian churches. For the time being we leave Geneva and continental Europe as a whole and, also the churches called "Reformed," in order to concentrate attention upon the mainstream of Presbyterian life as it developed in the English speaking world. This means that we will center our thought very especially on Presbyterianism in the British Isles and the United States of America. Apart from the perspective which this brief historical excursion should provide, attention will be drawn to some issues and tensions, to certain experiences and emphases, which will help us to achieve an understanding of the Presbyterian witness through the centuries and of problems which have never ceased to dog its path.

THE REFORMATION IN SCOTLAND

In the year 1560 the Scottish Reformation was consummated. Under the leadership of John Knox, who as an exile in Geneva had studied with Calvin, and ministered to a congregation of English speaking people in that city, the Roman Catholic Church was disestablished in Scotland. A new church, the Church of Scotland, Protestant in spirit, Calvinistic in doctrine and Presbyterian in structure, came into being. This church whose leaders had covenanted "to procure by all possible means, that the truth of God's Word may have free passage within this realm—and to put away all things that dishonour His name, that God may be truly and purely worshipped," was in due course recognized by Parliament as "the reformed Church of Scotland, the only true and holy kirk of Jesus Christ within this realm."

In that same year, 1560, was issued the *Scotch Confession of Faith*. This famous document, too long forgotten even in Scotland, but which guided the Scottish church for almost a century, until replaced later by the *Westminster Confession of Faith*, is a truly remarkable document. It is striking from both a Presbyterian and an ecumenical point of view. A well-known church historian has characterized it thus: "The *Confession* itself contains the truths common to the Reformed creeds of the Reformation. It contains all the ecumenical doctrines, as they have been called, that is, the truths taught in the early Ecumenical Councils and embodied in the Apostles' and Nicene Creeds; and adds those doctrines of grace, of pardon and of enlightenment through Word and Spirit, which were brought into special prominence by the Reformation revival of religion."

Soon after the publication of the *Confession*, there appeared a book designed to guide the new Scottish Church in matters relating to the organization of the church and the conduct of its life. This remarkable document is known as *The First Book of Discipline*.

A new Scotland was created, the spirit of whose people was destined to leave a lasting imprint upon Presbyterianism. The church of John Knox became the chief fountain from which streams of Presbyterian influence circulated throughout the English speaking world. It was, therefore, most fitting that the First General Council of the World Presbyterian Alliance should be held in the city of Edinburgh in 1877. The celebration in 1960, in this same historic capital of the Fourth Centennial of the Reformation in Scotland, will be a notable occasion. An opportunity will be provided not only to consider the religious debt which world Christianity owes to the Scottish Reformation, but also and in particular, to emphasize what Scottish Presbyterianism in its diverse epochs and emphases has meant to the Presbyterian churches of the world.

During the first century of the Reformation in Scotland, repeated attempts were made by the State to control the Church. Efforts were instituted to impose prelatic control upon the new democratic order. The practice of liturgical forms alien to the Church's own usage and tradition was enforced. The consequence was a revolt of the Presbyterian clergy and laity which led to the signing in 1638 of an epoch-making document called *The National Covenant*. In the venerated and picturesque graveyard that surrounds the historic church of the Greyfriars in Edinburgh, Scottish Presbyterians both from among the lordly and the lowly of the land made a solemn pledge, some of them inscribing their signatures with their blood. They swore to dedicate themselves to "The preservation of the Reformed Religion in the Church of Scotland, in doctrine, worship, discipline and government according to the Word of God and the example of the best Reformed churches." It was the determination of those sons of the early Reformers, as expressed in other documents of the period, that Christ should "bear the glory of ruling His own Kingdom and Church." For "there is no absolute and undoubted authority in the world excepting the authority of Christ the King, to whom it belongeth as properly to rule the Kirk according to the good pleasure of His own will, as it belongeth to Him to save the

Kirk by the merit of His own suffering." It was at the same time the aspiration of those men that the state too should be reformed and be a "servant of the blessed and only Potentate."

Now those men were not religious fanatics; they had a wide and informed outlook upon the affairs of state as well as upon the welfare and unity of the church. They were, as an eminent student of the epoch has well said, "not narrow, sectarian, bigoted, but large, liberal, catholic." Many a time in the future history of Presbyterianism were to be heard the notes sounded by that generation of men and women in their great religious struggle.

THE "SUBORDINATE STANDARDS"

The outstanding event in Presbyterian annals is the publication of the *Westminster Confession of Faith*. In this historic document is found the formulation of theological belief and ecclesiastical practice which has guided Presbyterian churches throughout the English speaking world, and which they have adopted, in some instances with modification, as their "subordinate standards." The *Westminster Confession* was the creation of an Assembly which was authorized by the English Parliament. Its sessions were held between 1643 and 1646 in a room in Westminster Abbey, London. Of the one hundred and fifty-one persons originally elected to membership by the churches, there were "ten Lords, and twenty commoners as lay assessors, and one hundred and twenty-one Divines." The vast majority of the members of the Westminster Assembly were English Puritans. Most of these men were Presbyterians. Included also, however, in the membership of the Assembly were several English Independents, or Congregationalists, and some Episcopalians. Among the Presbyterians were four ministers and two elders of the Church of Scotland.

From time to time, as we proceed, we shall have occasion to refer to some of the basic tenets of this Charter of Presbyterianism. For the moment let this observation suffice. Many of the controversies and growing pains of Presbyterian bodies in the last three hundred years have centered upon the way in which churches have defined their relationship to the *Westminster Confession of Faith,* to the *Directory for Church Government* and the *Larger and Shorter Catechisms* that were issued with it. It is important also to recall that, as soon as the "Westminster Standards" were completed, they were adopted by the Church of Scotland and so superseded the *Scottish Confession of Faith* of 1560. The formal title of this famous century-old *Scottish Confession* was "The Confession of the Faith and Doctrine believed and professed by the Protestants of Scotland."

PRESBYTERIANS MOVE INTO THE WORLD

Now comes the movement of Presbyterians into the world. It is estimated that of the total number of English Puritans who found their way to America, beginning with the voyage of the *Mayflower* which landed at Plymouth Rock in 1620, some twenty per cent were Presbyterians. They were noted for their warm evangelical piety. Their immediate descendants were destined to exert a deep influence on Presbyterianism when it became formally organized in the United States.

"PRESBYTER OF CHRIST IN AMERICA"

It was not from Scotland or England, however, but from Ulster in Ireland that the man came who helped to establish Presbyterianism in the New World. He was a young Irish pastor of Scottish descent, educated in the University of Glasgow, named Francis Makemie. After Makemie had labored several years in Maryland where he founded several congregations, he and three fellow pastors, also Scotch-Irish, gave Presbyterianism its first organized start in the United States. In the year 1706 a Presbytery was established in the city of Philadelphia.

Francis Makemie was a very remarkable pioneer, a servant of Christ in the best Pauline tradition. He was a dedicated pastor and evangelist who had much spiritual fruit to show for his labors. Like St. Paul, in order not to be burdensome to the people to whom he ministered, he supported himself. This he did in great part by his farming efforts.

True Calvinist, also, that he was, the young Presbyterian pastor insisted upon his freedom to preach the Gospel whenever and wherever the need and opportunity appeared. Because of his evangelistic endeavors in the area of New York, he was on one occasion put in prison by the Colonial authorities. He was charged with failing to possess a recognized license to preach. Though Makemie was finally acquitted by a jury, the case caused such a furor in the Colonies, and such concern in England, that the Governor was recalled. The Makemie trial greatly contributed to the cause of freedom of speech and the separation of Church and State in America.

That distinguished Presbyterian layman of a later generation, scholar, poet and diplomat, Henry Van Dyck, has dedicated to Francis Makemie the following stanza. The lines were first read at a celebration in Philadelphia commemorating the Two Hundredth Anniversary of the organization of the first Presbytery in the Americas. The stanza reads thus:

"Francis Makemie, Presbyter of Christ in America 1683-1708"

> To thee plain hero of a rugged race,
> We bring a meed of praise too long delayed,
> Oh, who can tell how much we owe to thee,
> Makemie, and to labors such as thine
> For all that makes America the shrine
> Of faith untrammeled and of conscience free?
> Stand here, graystone, and consecrate the sod,
> Where sleeps this brave Scotch-Irish man of God"

THE LOG COLLEGE

Within a decade of the organization of the first Presbytery, there came into being the first Presbyterian college in the New World. Its lowly rustic form appeared on the banks of the Neshaminy Creek in Pennsylvania, northeast of the city of Philadelphia. A Scotch-Irish pastor, William Tennent, founded what became known as the Log College. The Log College, a small wooden shack, twenty feet square, provided a classroom where Tennent, the local minister, tutored a group of young men for the ministry. These included his own four sons, who were apparently tutored in the home.

In the course of some years the College graduated eighteen students. Amid the simplicity of this sylvan environment, these new Presbyterian pastors and evangelists received an education which combined Biblical and Humanistic studies in the best Reformed tradition. They were nurtured in the heritage of warm-hearted piety and love of learning which had been the hallmark of John Calvin and John Milton, and which was destined to distinguish the life of that New England Presbyterian pastor, Jonathan Edwards, true mystic and profound metaphysician, who became President of the College of New Jersey. The important thing to remember is that the Log College men represented classical Presbyterianism in its finest form. In common with their Massachusetts contemporary, Edwards, they welcomed the advent and supported the work of the Episcopalian, George Whitfield, the father of the Great Awakening. In a time of barren legalistic orthodoxy and rigid ecclesiasticism, which have appeared from time to time in the course of Presbyterian history, they consistently stood for a personal experience of Christ and the reality of the "new man in Christ." They were partisans of a rich Biblicism, a competent theological understanding and a love of the Humanities.

The Log College achieved two things of supreme importance. First, it created a dynamic type of minister. Second, it inspired the founding of another college which was destined to become a leading fountain of American freedom and one of the chief glories of American education.

CRADLE OF CHURCHMEN AND STATESMEN

In 1746 was founded the College of New Jersey, now Princeton University. Its founders were a group of Presbyterian graduates of Yale University. The refusal of the Yale authorities to reinstate and graduate one of their own brilliant students, David Brainerd, because of a disparaging remark he made in private regarding the religion, or the lack of religion, of one of his teachers—although he afterwards expressed profound regret for having made the unworthy statement—led the men in question to found a new college.

While the College of New Jersey never belonged officially to the Presbyterian Church, it was closely related to the growing Church and actually educated its ministry. In the direction of its affairs from 1746 to this day, Presbyterian influence has predominated. What constituted, however, the most unique feature of the College of New Jersey at the time it was founded was this: it was the first intercolonial and interdenominational institution of learning in the history of the United States.

While all the presidents of Princeton University have been Presbyterian, three of them, one in each century since its founding, are linked in history to events which belong to the very soul of Presbyterianism. In the eighteenth century, President John Witherspoon was the only clergyman who signed the Declaration of American Independence. In the nineteenth century, President James McCosh was the earliest advocate of creating an organ to unite Presbyterians on a world basis. In the twentieth century Woodrow Wilson, who retired from the Presidency of Princeton University in order to enter politics, was the creator of the League of Nations. Political freedom, confessional solidarity with an ecumenical spirit, and international order are all rooted in a common theological heritage. They have all belonged in a very real sense to the "Presbyterian Way."

While Presbyterians were still the largest and most closely knit group in Colonial America, and before the first Presbytery was organized on the western side of the Alleghenies, the War of Independence began. Presbyterian involvement in the great struggle was both massive and decisive. The American Revolution has been called in fact a "Presbyterian Rebellion." For the backbone of Washington's forces was made up of

Scotch-Irish Presbyterians from New Jersey and Pennsylvania. There were understandable reasons why Presbyterians from Scotland and Ireland were so violently anti-British. They, or their forbears, had suffered grievously at the hands of the State. They were embittered because of past memories, and they resolved that, if they could prevent it, a similar situation would not be allowed to prevail in the Western World. So they rallied to the standard of revolt, and gave their substance, their thought and their lives to the creation of a new order. Later, when the Revolutionary struggle came to an end, the first church body to recognize the new order was the Presbytery of Hanover, in Virginia.

The part played by Presbyterians in the War of Independence and in the creation of the American Republic finds another symbol in the unique historic role of the College of New Jersey and its graduates in relation to the Constitution of the United States. I have already stated that Witherspoon was at the heart of the revolutionary movement. He was actually the only clergyman who was a member of the Continental Congress and the sole clerical signatory of the Declaration of Independence. A study of the identity and background of the men who drafted the Constitution of the United States gives this interesting result. Among them were four graduates of Yale, three of Harvard, one each from the Colleges of Columbia and Pennsylvania, while nine, including James Madison, were graduates of the small Presbyterian College of New Jersey.

CHURCH EXPANSION AND CONSOLIDATION

The Presbyterian march toward the West and into the South was going steadily forward in the years before the Revolution and greatly increased thereafter. In 1766 the Alleghenies were crossed and in 1781 was organized the Presbytery of Redstone in the Ohio Valley, a region which became known as "Presbyterian Valley." Eight years later, and while the western movement was in full progress, an epoch-making event took place in the city of Philadelphia. The first General Assembly of the Presbyterian Church was organized by the Synod of Philadelphia and New York. The Assembly convened under the Moderatorship of the redoubtable John Witherspoon. With this Assembly the first interstate religious body in American history came into being.

In its organization and development American Presbyterianism showed a spirit of independence together with a capacity for adaptation in the best Genevan tradition. Local congregations and Presbyteries enjoyed greater freedom and responsibility than was the case in Scotland. This was natural. Scottish Presbyterianism had been organized from the top down, the General Assembly being the first church judicatory to be created by Parliament at the time of the Reformation and charged with the organization of church life. American Presbyterianism, on the other hand, was organized from the bottom up. First came local congregations, then Presbyteries; Synods followed, and last came the General Assembly. This historical circumstance is responsible for the fact, which will be duly considered in the course of our study, that in American Presbyterianism the General Assembly does not possess the same kind of authority that it does in Scottish Presbyterianism.

Several events of importance, most of them inspiring but some of them tragic and depressing, marked the expansion and growth of the new Presbyterian Church. The spirit of missionary enthusiasm ran high. Through the union of some earlier missionary efforts a United Foreign Missionary Society was founded in 1817. Particularly devoted to the cause of missionary responsibility at home and abroad were the church's women. "The Female Cent Societies" of that period became the mother and inspirer of Presbyterian benevolences as they were to be developed down the years.

One of the earliest beneficiaries of the new fund was an institution established in 1812 in a small New Jersey town. This institution was officially named "The Theological Seminary of the Presbyterian Church in the United States of America located at Princeton in the state of New Jersey." It took over from the College of New Jersey the task of turning out ministers for Presbyterian parishes. As the years went by this Seminary sent out well-trained pastors and missionary pioneers for the frontiers of the Kingdom at home and abroad. Archibald Alexander, Samuel Miller and Charles Hodge were the Seminary's big three in the first decades of its life. Those truly great men communicated to successive generations of Princeton Seminary students fervent piety, missionary zeal, sound theological learning and an ecumenical spirit.

According to a contemporary Norwegian historian of the History of Missions, Princeton Seminary was the first theological college in the world to institute a lectureship on missions. This was done in the thirties of the nineteenth century. In the fifties of the century three young men were students on the seminary campus at the same time who were destined to become epoch-making missionary pioneers. Ashbel Green Simonton carried the Gospel to Brazil, becoming the founder of the Brazilian Presbyterian Church. Daniel MacGillway went as a missionary to Siam, now Thailand, where he established the first Evangelical community in that country. The third, Sheldon Jackson, well-named "The Little Giant," became the outstanding missionary pioneer of the American Northwest. He was the founder of many churches in that region and carried the Gospel beyond the Canadian Commonwealth to Alaska. By the mid-fifties of the century, on the eve of a great church union, Presbyterian congregations were to be found in every state in the Union. Their total membership was some four million. A million more were members of sister churches that bore the name Reformed instead of Presbyterian. Presbyterianism's largest Presbytery was now located on the Pacific Coast in Los Angeles, California.

This was the tale of Presbyterian and Reformed Churches in the United States until 1958, the year when a significant union took place between two leading Presbyterian denominations. At the beginning of that historic year eight different denominations bore the name of "Presbyterian." The largest of these was called "The Presbyterian Church in the United States of America." The second largest, which separated from the parent body as a result of the Civil War, taking the name of "The Presbyterian Church in the United States," is popularly known as "The Southern Presbyterian Church." In the South are also located two other Presbyterian Churches. One of these is called the "Associate Reformed Presbyterian Church." It represents a continuation in the Western world of a body of earnest Christians who seceded from the Church of Scotland in the eighteenth century. The other is The Cumberland Presbyterian Church, whose congregations are found mostly in the Cumberland Valley in Tennessee and the mid-south. They are the successors of a body of Presbyterians of great evangelistic fervor, who becoming impatient with standards of ministerial training which appeared to them to hinder the Church's advance at a crucial time, separated themselves from the parent body in 1806. The "United Presbyterian Church of North America" was formed when a union took place between two small Presbyterian churches in the United States which had been formed by the sons and daughters of staunch Presbyterians of Scottish origin. In the middle of the eighteenth century, their ancestors separated on conscientious grounds from the mother Church of Scotland. Another denomination, "The Reformed Presbyterian Church," represents those who felt that if they became part of the merger to which I have just referred they could not be loyal to the witness of the Scottish Covenanters from whom they are descended. This Church continues to stand for the principle that the state should officially acknowledge the Kingship of Jesus Christ, the historic position for which the Covenanters lived and died. In 1958, in the old Presbyterian city of Pittsburgh, two of these six churches, "The Presbyterian Church U.S.A." and "The United Presbyterian Church of North America" became one and formed Presbyterianism's largest denomination, "The United Presbyterian Church in the United States of America."

All of the Churches just mentioned are members of the

World Presbyterian Alliance. Together they constitute, with "The Presbyterian Church of Canada" and "The United Church of Canada," the "North American Area" of the Alliance. Two other Churches, not Presbyterian in name, but Reformed in their heritage, are also members of the Alliance. These are "The Reformed Church in America," formerly "The Dutch Reformed Church," and "The Evangelical and Reformed Church" composed of a union of two Churches which had their origin in Germany. The last mentioned body has recently united with "The Congregational Christian Church" to form "The United Church of Christ."

Outside this close knit fellowship of Presbyterian and Reformed Churches in the United States are some Presbyterian and Reformed Churches which hold themselves rigorously aloof from the main body of the churches which stem from the heritage of John Calvin and John Knox. They are the "Christian Reformed Church," "The Orthodox Presbyterian Church," and "The Bible Presbyterian Church." These churches which are small offshoots from two other Churches of the Reformed family, came into being as a result of very bitter theological controversy. Internationally they are members of the Reformed Ecumenical Synod.

THE DISCIPLINE OF DISUNITY

This tale of Presbyterian diversity and disunity during a period of American history shows that shadow as well as sunshine marked the path of Reformed Christianity in the United States. I refer to the shadow for a purpose. It is a shadow that has trailed the witness of Presbyterianism through the centuries. It has kept it penitent and humble, sensitive to human issues, and dependent upon the grace of God as it has gone crusadingly forward.

By focusing attention at this stage upon historical issues that have sometimes divided Presbyterians, the way will be prepared for a more intelligent understanding of Presbyterianism as a contemporary religious reality in this country and the world. While detailed historical survey is not the object of this book, but rather an interpretation of that which is natively and abidingly Presbyterian, together with a description and appraisal of Presbyterianism today, an important fact must not be forgotten. There have emerged on the highways and by-ways of Presbyterian history both conflicts and concerns which have a message for the present, not only for Presbyterians but also for all Christians.

In the early years of the nineteenth century when the great movement towards the West began to become intense and a wide field for evangelization was opened up among the thousands of Colonists already settled, and other thousands on trek to the frontiers of the nation, a very unhappy controversy arose in Presbyterian ranks. Some Presbyterians felt that the situation was so crucial and yet so transient that the requirements for ordination should, temporarily at least, be relaxed in order to provide a greater supply of recruits for the Church's ministry. The Church as a whole, moved by what it considered loyalty to the Reformed conception of an educated ministry, refused to modify its standards under any circumstances.

Two things happened. First, another church, the Cumberland Presbyterian Church, came into being. It was formed by ministers and laymen who put the immensity of human need for the Gospel before the proprieties of academic achievement on the part of those who proclaimed it. In the years that followed, the Cumberland Presbyterian Church added many thousands of new members to its fellowship, while the mother Church in that period, lacking an adequate number of missionary recruits, became relatively stagnant. Second, the Presbyterian Church lost the new American frontier to Baptists and Methodists. These were not concerned at that time about educational standards for their missionary evangelists and circuit riders.

Many Presbyterians today, who, under all normal conditions, are committed to the necessity of a highly educated ministry, give thanks to God for those Baptists and Methodists who evangelized the expanding frontiers of the nation in a crucial hour. They are no less grateful to the clear visioned, passionate hearted men of Cumberland, who were truer to a native, but oft forgotten strain in the Genevan and Scottish tradition, than were the Presbyterian ecclesiastics of that day. In consequence, however, of its academic rigidity in the presence of a missionary situation, the Presbyterian Church, which was the strongest religious body in Colonial America and in the early days of the Republic, was forced in the early decades of the nineteenth century to yield ground to other denominations.

From the time of its establishment in America, Presbyterianism has manifested a tension between strongly divergent viewpoints and emphases. This tension has affected both the church polity and the devotional spirit of Presbyterians. There have been American Presbyterians so rigidly theological in their temperament and outlook, that they have tended to convert ideas into divinities. They have made their views about the great Christian realities a substitute for the reality of their own relationship to Christ and the new life in Him. There have been those also who have tended to be disdainful of doctrine, failing to realize its living and abiding importance for the illumination and strengthening of life. Most Presbyterians, however, both among the clergy and the laity, have been loyal to the great central tradition. They have sought to combine in their life and witness a balanced concern for doctrine and life, for piety and learning, for personal religion and social concern, for loyalty to tradition and to the challenge of contemporary history.

While this is true the emergence of deep conscientious divergencies between Presbyterian and Presbyterian has led, at different times, to the formation in the United States of mutually antagonistic parties within the Church. Thus we find the "Old Side" and the "New Side" the "Old Lights" and the "New Lights" and later the "Old School" and the "New School." So militant and divisive became the standpoints of the "Old School" and the "New School" in the first half of the nineteenth century that from 1838 to 1869 the Presbyterian Church

U.S.A. had two General Assemblies, each of which claimed to be the true mother church. This unhappy division took place at the very time when unity and the coordination of policy and effort were most needed because of the westward expansion! Fortunately, however, as an expression of what is also a Presbyterian tradition, the two Assemblies became reunited, after thirty-one years of separation.

Creative controversy continued from time to time. But the Church had matured and was in a period of great expansion when suddenly the Civil War broke out. This most tragic occurrence in the life of the American Nation divided the churches as it divided the country. Of the major denominations only the Episcopalians, who have had a traditional capacity for maintaining ecclesiastical unity, were not rent in twain. Two Presbyterian churches emerged from the bloody conflict. Repeated negotiations have sought to bring these two churches together. They are completely one in faith and life, in history and tradition, but thus far all efforts to reunite them have failed. Happily, however, despite the situation created among the rank and file of the beloved sister church in the South by psychological and sociological factors, due in no small degree to the Supreme Court's decision on the racial issue, the two major Presbyterian churches in the United States are closely united in spirit and relationships. Both are members of the National Council of Churches, of the World Presbyterian Alliance, and of the World Council of Churches. On the great frontiers of the Kingdom, moreover, in Korea and Brazil, for example, both bodies are cooperatively related to the same national church.

The most recent phase of bitter strife by which the Presbyterian Church was rent and which, in God's providence, prepared it for the greatest creative period in its history, occurred in the early decades of the present century. The basic issues centered in the authority of the General Assembly. Apart from the sanction of Presbyteries, did the General Assembly have authority at any given meeting to interpret the Church's faith and to establish norms of loyalty to its historic standards, *The Westminster Confession of Faith and Cate-*

chisms? Involved in this controversy was a totally unPresbyterian view of the meaning of the Church, and also an attitude toward the status of doctrinal formulation and the legitimate difference of opinion among Christians, which violated the genius of the Reformed faith.

In the thirties "The Presbyterian Church in the U.S.A." became divided. After years of bitter controversy, the dissident party under the leadership of a distinguished New Testament scholar, J. Graham Machen, of Princeton Theological Seminary, established a new seminary, a new Board of Foreign Missions, and eventually a new Church. In the course of a few years this new church became two miniature churches, each with its own seminary, its own Board of Missions and its own national and international relationships. The first-formed of these churches adopted the name of "The Orthodox Presbyterian Church," and its offshoot, "The Bible Presbyterian Church." This latter body has become still further divided.

THE ACHIEVEMENT OF DYNAMIC UNITY

The experience of division, just described, became in God's providence the prelude to a great quickening in the life of "The Presbyterian Church in the U.S.A." The same has happened in the Southern Presbyterian Church, which fortunately has been able to deal with dissension without becoming divided. The past two decades are rightly regarded as one of the most creative periods in the history of the Church to which I have the honor of belonging. Many things have happened. Inspired by a new interest in Bible study and theology, and sensitive to the necessity of communicating the Christian faith more effectively, steps were taken to issue more adequate curriculum materials for the Church's Sunday Schools. Under the leadership of the Board of Christian Education, there was developed "The New Curriculum." Its appearance marked the beginning of a new epoch in the Sunday School world. Under the same auspices, leadership was given in the field of

Christian literature. The Westminster Press was created. A new pace was set among the Churches of the nation by the publication of *The Westminster Study Bible* and important illustrative material for Biblical research. A Council on Theological Education was created. The seminaries of the denomination, which had hitherto been virtual waifs so far as official denominational support was concerned, now participated in the Church's General Benevolence Budget.

At the same time the Board of National Missions took the initiative in launching an aggressive evangelistic effort called "The New Life Movement," Calvin's famous crest was its emblem. A flaming heart in the open hand, interpreted by the motto, "My heart I give Thee, Lord, eagerly and sincerely," led to a deepened devotion. A general "Forward Movement" was launched. At the close of the War a "Restoration Fund" was created for the advancement of missionary activity, the establishment of new churches, and the support of theological education. The Church's General Council was reorganized and was vested with effective powers to provide dynamic and effective leadership in the Church's life. One phase of the Council's leadership was the issuing in the darkest hour of the McCarthy era the document known as "A Letter to Presbyterians." This Letter which had great national and international repercussions, was in due course endorsed by the General Assembly.

In those crucial and creative years an advance was also made in the sphere of religious journalism, at both the theological and popular levels. Under the leadership of a group of Presbyterians, there came into being a quarterly review called *Theology Today*. In the sixteen years of its history *Theology Today* has attained a larger circulation and perchance a greater influence than any similar theological quarterly in the world. A few years later the century-old *Presbyterian*, a church weekly which had served and weathered many different phases of the Church's pilgrimage, gave place to *Presbyterian Life*. This fortnightly magazine, brilliantly edited by a group of younger Presbyterians, most of whom are members of the laity, has, in the judgment of competent authorities, made history in the field of religious journalism. More copies of *Presbyterian Life* are printed each fortnight than of any denominational paper today.

Some events occurred which gave new and significant meaning to unity and stirred afresh the Presbyterian soul toward mission. The Presbyterian Church in the U.S.A. and the United Presbyterian Church in North America became one body in June 1958, constituting the United Presbyterian Church in the U.S.A. The very first action of the Uniting General Assembly was to issue a document entitled "In Unity for Mission."

As an expression of the great advance and newborn spirit, the boards of foreign missions and committees on inter-church relations of the uniting churches were merged under the significant title "The Commission on Ecumenical Missions and Relations." The fulfillment of the Church's mission to the world and the pursuit of Christian unity in the world would henceforth have a common direction.

The following year the announcement of a series of anniversaries awoke the newly united church, as well as other Presbyterian Churches throughout the nation and the world, to a fresh sense of heritage from the past and responsibility in the present. Presbyterians have been stirred by memories of Calvin and Geneva, of the founding of the Reformed Church of France, the celebration of the Church of Scotland under John Knox, and the first centennial of the National Presbyterian Church of Brazil, a most glorious fruit of missionary labor.

These memories and the meeting in São Paulo, Brazil, of the Eighteenth General Council of the Alliance of Reformed Churches holding the Presbyterian Order have awakened among Presbyterians everywhere a new interest in their religious heritage. No time, therefore, could be more opportune than the present to offer to Presbyterians, to other Christians, and to the public in general, an interpretation of what is meant by "The Presbyterian Way of Life."

✛ 2 ✛

A Theologically
Minded People

C HRISTIAN churches, like all human groups, have their characteristic features. This is true whether they be local congregations, national denominations or world confessional bodies. They have in common, of course, those essential things which derive directly from Christ, and without which they would not be Christian at all. Apart from that, however, a Christian church, whatever its dimension or name, bears the unmistakable marks of the racial inheritance, as well as the historical experience and the theological outlook of its members. Especially important in this regard are the founding members who gave the church its tradition, and those leaders who subsequently shaped its course in crucial moments of its life.

THE PRESBYTERIAN SOUL

In a very real sense, there is a Presbyterian soul as there is an Anglican soul, a Lutheran soul, a Methodist, a Roman Catholic, and an Eastern Orthodox soul. It is no less true that the soul of a church undergoes a change through a deeper experience of Christ, a truer understanding of Christ or a sacrificial

34

witness to Christ in an hour of special challenge. For all churches have their "human," often their all too "human" side, as well as that loyalty which makes them Christian and churches of God. In other words, what a church is and does in certain situations may be determined by factors which are neither Christian nor theological. Before I deal, therefore, with the theological mindedness of Presbyterians, let me refer briefly to one of those non-theological factors which has had a basic influence upon the development of Presbyterianism in the United States. Consideration of this matter may shed light upon some episodes to which reference was made in Chapter One.

So far as American Presbyterianism is concerned, its main ethnic stock in the decisive period of its formation was Scottish. This stock was represented especially by those sons of Scotland who migrated in the seventeenth century to Northern Ireland, many of whose descendants later crossed the Atlantic and are known in American history as Scotch Irish.

Students of racial psychology have drawn attention to the fact that there is in the Scottish temperament, when unmoved, a certain impassiveness. When, however, the soul of the Scot has been roused, this native impassiveness gives place to a passionate absolutism, to a fanatical extremism in both ideas and loyalties. It was an Englishman, the famous essayist, Charles Lamb, who thus described the denizens of Britain's northern territory, "When once they adopt a decided attitude, you never catch the Caledonian mind in an undress. The Caledonian never hints or suggests anything but unloads his ideas in perfect order and completion. He has no falterings of self-suspicion. The twilight of dubiety never falls upon him. Is he orthodox, he has no doubt. Is he an infidel, he has none either. Between the affirmative and the negative there is no border land with him. You cannot hover with him upon the confines of truth."

In the possession of this particular trait, the Scot is remarkably akin to what the Spaniard was in the days of Spain's greatness. For both, when deeply stirred, the truth has been a "yes" or a "no," with no place for nuances or middle ground. In this respect Scots and Spaniards have been unlike the English and the French. In order to understand how this could be, we need only recall that in the racial composition of the Spanish and Scottish peoples there is a common Celtic strain. Frenchmen and Englishmen have had a native capacity to see shades of truth and to adopt mediating positions. Not so the Spaniards and the Scots with their hot Celtic blood.

There is a musical instrument which is a perfect symbol of the point I am making. The bagpipe is common to northern Spain, to Ireland, and to Scotland. Now in Scottish history and tradition, this instrument of music has never been used to express life's ordinary work-a-day emotions, nor has it ever been used to accompany congregational singing on a Sunday. It has never, in fact, been used in religious services at all, as have the harp and the trumpet, the organ and the violin, whether alone or in unison. The bagpipe has been used rather to interpret or arouse the great frontier emotions of grief, mirth and crusading devotion. Bagpipes are blown to skirl a dirge of sorrow at a funeral, to stir hilarity at a dance, and to impassion the hearts of soldiers on the march or before a battle. But bagpipe strains, which the Celtic soul of the writer loves above all the music on earth, have never been domesticated, nor baptized into Christ.

Why have I made this diversion, sauntering into the realms of racial psychology and music? I have done so because there is ground for affirming that some of the most glorious episodes in the history of Scotch, Irish, and American Presbyterianism, as well as some of the most unhappy, have owed not a little to the Celtic capacity for passion and extremes. For obvious reasons I will refrain from alluding to the many creative contributions which men and women of Scotch or Scotch-Irish descent have made to the "Presbyterian Way" in the United States and to American life in general. Caledonian achievements in this regard are part of the historical record. My mood and intention are quite different. I feel somewhat as

the citizens of Geneva, those loyal and adoring sons of John
Calvin must have felt, when they erected the expiatory monument to Servetus, to which reference was made in the preceding chapter. Calvin was the child of his time, as well as the
greatest churchman and scholar of his generation. The "Presbyterian Way" in American history has been marked by great-
heartedness and vision. It has been marked also at certain
points on the road by some displays of narrowness and extremism, of schismatic complacency and dogmatic self-righteousness. These traits were not derived from the Bible or from
Jesus Christ, nor yet from John Calvin or John Knox, but from
a recognized element of weakness in a great race. But, happily,
the mother race of St. Columba of Erin and Iona, and of
John Witherspoon of Paisley and Princeton, mingled with
Presbyterian Puritans from England and Wales, and with Reformed cousins from France and Switzerland, from Germany
and Holland, from Hungary and Czechoslovakia, to form in
one great orchestral harmony the Presbyterian and Reformed
family in the United States of America.

PRESBYTERIAN PASSION FOR TRUTH

Presbyterianism, more perhaps than any other Protestant
confession, has emphasized the importance of loving God with
the mind. The Reformed tradition to which Presbyterianism
belongs has manifested throughout its history a passion for ob-
jectivity, a striving to grasp and to express in intellectual terms
the meaning and implications of its faith. A passionate concern
about Truth has been and continues to be a characteristic aspect of the "Presbyterian Way."

This concern is part of the Calvinistic legacy of Presbyterians. Few men in Christian history have manifested such a
sense of the majesty of Truth as John Calvin. Both Luther and
Calvin passed through profound experiences of conversion
which shaped their life and work. Whereas Luther, however,
experienced the reality of rebirth in the healing of his
wounded spirit with the balsam of a Bible verse, "The just

shall live by faith," Calvin's experience of renewal was different. In the heyday of his self-satisfied humanistic career, he felt himself imperiously grasped by a gracious and almighty Hand. He was overwhelmed with a sense of God's sovereign grace. It was natural that Luther should tend to concentrate on the subjective, personal side of Christianity, giving utterance to his feeling in matchless hymns. Out of Lutheranism came the sublime music of Bach and that creative, spiritual phenomenon which we call German Pietism. Calvin on the other hand, following an overwhelming encounter with a Sovereign Being who demanded his heart and to whom he gave it in flaming devotion, turned his thoughts to the objective reality of God and His Grace. He began to look at life in all its phases in the light of God and His sovereign purpose for mankind.

This does not mean that Calvin, the humanist, who was interested and continues to the end of his life to be interested in "truth from any quarter," had not previously been wrestling with the question of man's relationship to God. Still less does it mean that after the great encounter took place Calvin was uninterested in the subjective aspect of Christian living, commonly called "piety." In one of his very rare references to his own spiritual experience, he strikes a most significant autobiographical note in his *Commentary on the Psalms*. Here are his words: "He subdued my heart (too hardened by age) to docility. Thus having acquired some taste of true piety I burned with such zeal to go forward that although I did not desist from other studies I yet pursued them more indifferently. Nor had a year gone by when all who were desirous of this purer doctrine thronged to me, novice and beginner that I was, in order to learn it." Elsewhere he exclaims, "Thou O Lord, didst shine upon me with the brightness of Thy Spirit."

This "purer doctrine" to which Calvin refers is the Biblical doctrine of the divine-human relationship and the new life as found in the Bible. In God's manifestation to him in Christ he found the Personal Truth. He understood that Truth through the illumination of the Holy Spirit. Out of this divine human encounter came his zeal for the study of the Scriptures and his sense of God's sovereignty in all human affairs. Having been made intensely aware that Truth is personal, edification, that is, becoming built up in Christ, became for Calvin the supreme practical criterion as to whether or not the Truth had been understood. Calvin was also destined to become the great theologian of the Holy Spirit, Who had illumined his understanding. His personal experience, and its subsequent fruits in his theological writing and public ministry, were to make an indelible imprint upon Reformed Christianity.

A fascinating and most enlightening comparison between Luther and Calvin in their common attempt to rediscover primitive Christianity was made many years ago by an Oxford scholar, A. M. Fairbairn. "The moving impulse was in Luther the sense of sin," says Principal Fairbairn, "But in Calvin the love of truth alike as ideal and as reality. Luther found in the sources a way of escape from sin, Calvin an ideal which men are bound to realize. Luther's passion was to believe and teach a true soteriology; Calvin's was to build a system and a state in the image of the truth of God. . . . It is characteristic that his fundamental thought is not as with Luther, justification by faith, or the mode in which the guilty man may be made right with God, but it is grace, or the absoluteness and supremacy of the will of God as the gracious will which purposes and achieves salvation. Justification by faith was, of course, as much an essential part of Christian faith for Calvin as for Luther. The difference between the two men is simply one of perspective and emphasis, resulting from their two different types of personal experience, each type being classically Christian, through which they individually passed."

RIVAL CRUSADERS FOR THE MIND OF MODERN MAN

The far-reaching significance for human life and history of a passion for truth, or theological mindedness, will become clear if I refer to three men whose lives were an incarnation of this passion, and who gave birth to three dynamic movements.

The first of these is Thomas Aquinas. The most potent intellectual movement in the Roman Catholic world today is inspired by the thought of the great Dominican monk of the thirteenth century who wrote the famous theological treatise called *Summa Theologica*. In the Protestant world only Calvin's *The Institutes of the Christian Religion* can be compared in massiveness and influence with this epoch-making classic. Today neo-Thomism represents a movement which grows in potency and importance. It is designed to rediscover the thought of St. Thomas and to apply it to the problems of our time in both the religious and secular realms. There is clear evidence that Calvin knew and appreciated the thought of Aquinas. A very distinguished former Dominican, now a professor of theology in a Presbyterian theological Seminary, and a profound student of St. Thomas and John Calvin, has made these observations in a still unpublished treatise. Says Dr. George A. Barrois of Princeton, "Aquinas is probably the outstanding representative of the theology of the Church prior to the eve of the Reformation and the Council of Trent. We are indebted to him for the most complete and systematic synthesis of Christian thought at a time when the Holy Scriptures were still regarded as the ultimate authority in matters of doctrine, and when tradition was not yet acknowledged in Rome as an independent channel of the divine revelation. It is our conviction that a diligent and careful study of Aquinas would lead to a better understanding of the positions of historical Calvinism, not only in its relation to Medieval expressions of the Christian faith, but in itself.

"Our conviction rests ultimately upon a very personal experience. After a long and intimate familiarity with St. Thomas and Thomism we were led, for 'the wind bloweth when it listeth,' to make Calvin and Calvinism the subject of our meditations. Instead of feeling estranged in this new atmosphere we discover between both systems of thought an amazing number of affinities which could not be regarded as merely casual. Even when Calvin opposes the tenets of the School he expresses himself in such terms as undoubtedly reveal his thorough knowledge of the position of his adversaries. Aquinas wanted to be an expositor of the Word, and his goal was to give primarily an articulate exposition of Christian beliefs."

In his penetrating study, the former disciple and continuing admirer of the great St. Thomas remarks, "We shall chart currents already perceptible in Aquinas and survey stepping stones toward the doctrines of the Reformation. Then we shall refrain from wholesale identification of the doctrine of Aquinas with modern Roman Catholic teaching. Neo-Thomists have pledged their adherence to recent dogmatic formulations and unconsciously read Aquinas in the light of the Council of Trent or of the Council of the Vatican. But Aquinas is a representative of the theology of the pre-Tridentine church and its homogeneous continuity down to our days is an unfounded assumption too easily challenged."

The bearing of these affirmations upon the present study is this: Calvinism, which alone can match Thomism as an attempt to understand Christian truth and to give it structural form, has certain affinities with the supreme theological creation of the Middle Ages. In the sphere of religious thought today Neo-Calvinism alone can be compared in significance with the popularity and power of neo-Thomism. Both represent attempts to find a theological basis for human thought and action, and to provide modern man in his brokenness and confusion with a Christian world view. While "neo-Calvinism" and that vague designation "neo-orthodoxy" are by no means synonymous with the Reformed Tradition to which Presbyterians belong, it is true that thinkers belonging to this tradition, such as Barth and Brunner, the Niebuhr brothers and Wilhelm Niessel, have led the van in an effort to develop a system of Christian truth for our time.

Another historic figure in the Roman tradition, and a contemporary of Calvin, who confronted the issue of truth in a confused time, and who crusaded for a solution totally different from that of Calvin, is Ignatius Loyola, the Spanish Basque. Educated in the same institution as Calvin, Loyola found the answer to all human questions regarding Truth in a blind absolute loyalty to the institutional Church as represented by the Roman See. His formula for all seekers and doubters is enshrined in that tremendous utterance, "Let us be like a dead body, which of itself is incapable of motion, or like a blind man's staff." For submission to the sovereign Lord Jesus Christ and to the truth of Holy Scripture in which Christ is revealed, the former knight-errant substituted allegiance to the Virgin Mother, Christ's continuing Representative "until He come," and to the Holy Roman Church as the absolute interpreter and executor in history of Christ's sovereign will. Today there is a neo-Jesuitism which happily adopts a very different approach to Protestant Christianity from that taken by the sixteenth century sons of Loyola who controlled the Council of Trent. It was they who made irreparable the rift which John Calvin would fain have healed, if the Roman Communion were willing to meet the demands of the Reformers. The present-day sons of Calvin, be they theologically Calvinists or neo-Calvinists, and ecclesiastically Reformed or Presbyterian, continue to have the same concern for Truth that marked the Genevan Doctor. Another mark, too, they share with the Society of Jesus. As the two great historic forces become aligned afresh to do battle for the Truth of Christ, each in accordance with its understanding of the Church of Christ, both are committed to the proposition that Truth demands absolute obedience, accompanied by action, on the part of all who profess it.

During the past hundred years, no secular thinker has so influenced the course of secular history as Karl Marx. This man achieved an ideological structure based upon the conviction that an inexorable, dialectical, impersonal movement in history would give the eventual victory to the World's Proletariat. Marx is the father of world Communism, Christianity's greatest rival in our time. Only a positive, constructive approach to Communism has the slightest chance of becoming its competitor for the world of tomorrow. Such an approach must be based upon an ideology, or rather a theology, which affirms with passionate conviction the reality of a divine eternal purpose whereby the living sovereign God guarantees the victory of His Elect. But who are God's Elect? They are all those who truly obey God and form part of His Church, which is the "Democracy of the Saints" and the Community of destiny. No theologian in history gave so central a place in his scheme of thought to the fact and implications of God's everlasting design for mankind as did John Calvin. This fact has great significance for Presbyterians today.

Why have I brought upon the stage the great figures of Aquinas, Loyola and Marx?

If the "Presbyterian Way" is to mean anything in this age, if Calvin's sons and daughters are to be worthy of their heritage and relevant to their time, they must grasp God's purpose and adjust themselves to it. Without necessarily accepting all his ideas, Presbyterians must follow the example of that great neo-Calvinist, Karl Barth. They must live with Eternal Truth. In every human situation, they must "do the Truth." In a word they must become servants of the Truth, doers of the Word as well as hearers of it.

In the Preface to the Fifth Edition of his epoch-making Commentary on the Epistle to the Romans, which began to restore the Bible to its rightful place in Christian thought, Barth quotes some lines of poetry from a German pastor, which, being translated, run thus:

"God needs men, not creatures
Full of noisy catchy phrases.
Dogs He asks for, who their noses
Deeply thrust into Today
And there scent Eternity.
Should it lie too deeply buried
Then go on, and fiercely burrow,
Excavate until Tomorrow."

Not only, however, must Presbyterians be diligent burrowers in the depths of Today in order to discern God's unchanging purpose for Tomorrow, they must never cease to tread the pilgrim way. He who finds the Truth must love it and obey it.

He must gird himself with the belt of Truth, wear unashamedly the badge of Truth, and, with the gait of a crusader, unfurl the banner of Truth.

"Scenting Eternity in Today," let thoughtful Presbyterians be inspired by the great contemporary quest for Truth to take seriously the significance for Christianity and the Christian Church in our time of the thought structures of Thomism, Jesuitism and Marxism. Let them at the same time explore afresh their own Calvinistic heritage of faith and rededicate themselves to the cause of Truth and Goodness in our time.

THE PRESBYTERIAN STANDARDS OF FAITH

To be a Presbyterian anywhere in the world is to belong to a community of Christians, large or small, who have adopted a common statement of belief. To this creedal statement, which is simple but basic in the case of ordinary church members, and more complex and theological in the case of ordained ministers and elders, Presbyterian loyalty is pledged. This means that all Presbyterians are members or officers of a Church which is founded upon a definite Constitution. This Constitution is authoritative for the faith and practice of local congregations, Presbyteries, Synods, together with the General Assembly and its related Boards and Agencies. In other words, Presbyterians belong to a confessional church, as distinguished from a Church denomination whose members are knit together at the congregational level, and who acknowledge no higher jurisdiction than that which is vested in the duly elected officers of the congregation.

The confessional or creedal statement, which forms the constitutional basis of Presbyterian Churches in the English speaking world, is the historic document referred to in Chapter One, which was drafted in London, England, in the seventeenth century, and is known as the *Westminster Confession of Faith*. Some Presbyterian Churches have been accustomed to include in their constitutions, as adjuncts to the Confession itself, two Catechisms, the Larger and Shorter Catechism. These Catechisms were drafted by the same Assembly of Divines who composed the *Westminster Confession*. In several Presbyterian churches, especially in the United States, the historic *Confession* has been modified, or supplementary articles have been added to it. In other Presbyterian churches acts approved by the Church's General Assembly have defined the precise interpretation which the denomination gives to formal subscription to the *Confession of Faith* on the part of ministers and elders.

Still other churches have included in their constitutional standards or published in official church literature, additional statements of belief. These are designed to interpret or simplify the traditional standards, without the basic doctrines being in any way affected. We find included, for example, in the Constitution of the recently formed "United Presbyterian Church in the United States of America," two statements one of which bears the title *A Brief Statement of the Reformed Faith,* the other *The Confessional Statement*. These are described as "Permissible and legitimate interpretations of the system of doctrine taught in Holy Scripture and formally set forth in the Westminster Standards." They are not to be regarded, however, as substitutes for, but supplements to the *Westminster Confession* and *Catechisms*. They are designed rather as popular summaries of the Church's faith, to be used for the instruction of Church members, especially the youth, who increasingly need a non-technical statement of what the Church believes. In every instance, however, it is made clear that the Westminster documents are the *subordinate standards* of the Church's faith and practice. The *supreme standard* of belief and behavior is Holy Scripture alone.

It will be of interest to the reader to have the exact text, with accompanying comments, of the "ordination vows" taken by ministers in some representative Presbyterian Churches today. I begin with Presbyterianism's largest denomination, "The United Presbyterian Church in the U.S.A." In this denomination the following questions relating to belief are addressed to all candidates for the ministry:

1. Do you believe in one God—Father Son and Holy Spirit— And do you confess anew the Lord Jesus Christ as your Saviour and Lord, and acknowledge Him Head over all things to the Church, which is His Body?
2. Do you believe the Scriptures of the Old and New Testaments to be the Word of God, the only infallible rule of faith and practice?
3. Do you sincerely receive and adopt the *Confession of Faith* and *Catechisms* of this Church as containing the system of doctrine taught in the Holy Scriptures?

Here are the corresponding questions relating to belief which must be answered in the affirmative by all ministers of the Church of Scotland. Let it be observed that the Church of Scotland, as now constituted, was formed in 1929 by a union of the then Church of Scotland and the United Free Church of Scotland. The questions run:

1. Do you believe in one God—Father Son and Holy Spirit; and do you confess anew the Lord Jesus Christ as your Saviour and Lord?
2. Do you believe the Word of God which is contained in the Scriptures of the Old and New Testaments, to be the supreme rule of faith and life?
3. Do you believe the fundamental doctrines of the Christian faith contained in the *Confession of Faith* of this Church?

The version of the questions which ministers of the Free Church of Scotland are required to answer is as follows:

1. Do you believe the Scriptures of the Old and New Testaments to be the Word of God and the only rule of faith and manners?
2. Do you sincerely own and believe the whole doctrine contained in the *Confession of Faith*, approved by

former General Assemblies of this Church, to be founded upon the Word of God; and do you acknowledge the same as the confession of your faith; and will you firmly and constantly adhere thereto, and to the utmost of your power assert, maintain, and defend the same, and the purity of worship as presently practised in this Church?

3. Do you disown all Popish, Socinian, Armenian, Erastian, and other doctrines tenets and opinions whatsoever, contrary to and inconsistent with, the foresaid *Confession of Faith?*"

A study of these three series of questions which, when answered in the affirmative constitute "ordination vows," suggests some basic observations.

First. The question regarding a minister's personal faith and commitment is omitted in the constitution of the Free Church of Scotland. It could be said, of course, that it ought to be taken for granted that a candidate for the Presbyterian ministry is a person who affirmed his personal faith in Jesus Christ, when he was admitted to Church membership. That is true, yet some remarks are in order. The declaration of faith in the Triune God, and of personal allegiance to Jesus Christ as "Saviour and Lord," is a most fitting avowal for a young man to make as he enters upon the great Apostolic succession of Christ's ministers. For a Presbyterian minister, moreover, such a declaration becomes a continuing echo of the impressive significance of John Calvin's crest with the flaming heart. "My heart I give Thee, Lord, eagerly and sincerely." The absence of a statement regarding personal relationship to Jesus Christ is in danger of reducing the ordination formula to a solemn but cold declaration of the acceptance of ideas regarding the Bible, and of doctrines founded upon the Bible, which are contained in a great historic compendium of Christian truth. Wherever and whenever a relationship to ideas about God, sound and orthodox though these may be, takes precedence over a relationship to the living, redeeming God Himself, we have an example of Presbyterian scholasticism. This phenomenon and its significance we shall have occasion to consider at a later stage in our study.

Second. The first two Churches above mentioned, by emphasizing "system of doctrine" or "fundamental doctrines" in their formulas of subscription for ordination, imply that every jot and tittle in their Confession of Faith is not to be regarded as equally authoritative and binding upon the conscience of those who sign it.

The United Presbyterian Church in the U.S.A., for example, requires the acceptance by all its ministers of the Confession of Faith and Catechisms of this Church as containing the "system of doctrine" taught in the Holy Scriptures. This is a matter upon which such stalwart Presbyterian theologians as Charles Hodge, A. A. Hodge, and Benjamin B. Warfield, whose classical orthodoxy no one can question, felt very strongly. For them as for other Presbyterians in the U.S.A. the Church's "secondary standards," being human documents, cannot be equated with Holy Scripture. They may contain things that are unfortunately expressed, or that do not belong to the *essence* of the Christian faith, and so are not part of the "system of doctrine" taught in the Holy Scriptures. In the Constitution of the United Presbyterian Church we find, accordingly, this very luminous and significant declaration: "The United Presbyterian Church in the United States of America, while adhering to the Westminster Confession of Faith and Catechisms, Larger and Shorter, herein set forth, as presenting the system of doctrine taught in the Scriptures, which are the supreme and only infallible rule of faith and practice, also, affirms, in conformity with the spirit of the Reformed faith, that it is the right and duty of a living Church to restate and interpret its faith as occasion may require, and as has been done by the Uniting Churches, so as to display in language currently understood, such fuller appreciation of Biblical truth as may have come to it under the guidance of the Holy Spirit."

The same concern to bring doctrinal standards into line with further insight into the Bible and Biblical truth which the Church, under the guidance of the Holy Spirit may have attained, and also to express Christian ideas in the living speech of men has manifested itself also in other Presbyterian Churches, especially the Church of Scotland. In the constitution of the Scottish Church the questions addressed to candidates for ordination are prefaced with this affirmation:

"The Church of Scotland holds as its subordinate standard the Westminster Confession of Faith, recognizing liberty of opinion on such points of doctrine as do not enter into the substance of the Faith, and claiming the right, in dependence upon the promised guidance of the Holy Spirit, to formulate, interpret, or modify its subordinate standards: always in agreement with the Word of God and the fundamental doctrines of the Christian Faith contained in the said Confession, of which agreement the Church itself shall be sole judge."

THE THEOLOGICAL RESPONSIBILITY OF A LIVING CHURCH

Around the question as to whether a living Church has the right and obligation, under the Spirit's guidance to reinterpret, rephrase, and supplement the confessional statement of its faith in loyalty to the Word of God, controversies have raged in Presbyterian history. They have rent many a church on both sides of the Atlantic, and in other parts of the world as well. Into the details of these struggles it is not necessary to enter. Suffice it to say that they were necessary and creative experiences. Passions may have been aroused, churches may have been divided, but the genius of the Reformed faith became clarified. Church bodies bearing the Presbyterian name became mellowed and mature. Their witness to Christ became more dynamic and united in the measure in which their understanding of the Bible and of Christ, and of their own heritage and role, was deepened.

Several factors have contributed to create a new solidarity among Presbyterians and Presbyterian Churches that have been through the fires of conflict in the last century and have been purified thereby. Outstanding has been the awareness that in the Christian tradition to which they belong continual renewal and reformation, according to the Word of God, is an imperious demand. In the early days of Reformed Christianity a slogan was sounded, *"Ecclesia reformata semper est reformanda,"* which being interpreted means "The Reformed Church must always be reforming." It was a famous Dutch theologian, Abraham Kuyper, who said that the trouble with the Reformed Church was not that it formulated new statements of faith, but that it failed to do so and was thus disloyal to its origin and nature. The day of Presbyterian scholasticism which would equate human ways of expressing the "truth as it is in Jesus" with that truth itself, is drawing to a close. The spirit which has consistently opposed any change whatever in the Westminster Confession of Faith or to the formula of subscription to it, sounding an "Everlasting no" to the slightest modification of the Church's Subordinate Standards, represents that native absolutism to which I have already referred as a point of weakness in the Celtic character. Such a spirit never did represent either the spirit of John Calvin or of John Knox.

Happily, in American Presbyterianism, from the time when the first General Assembly was constituted in 1788, the Church's officers, both lay and clerical, were committed only to the "system of doctrine" contained in the Westminster Confession. They were not committed to accept every detail in the document, and were given a certain freedom in defining the structure and dimension of the "system of doctrine" itself. When, therefore, it was proposed many years ago that the American Presbyterian Church should pass a "Declaratory Act," as had been done by the Free Church of Scotland in 1892, in order to redefine the meaning of subscription to the Confession of Faith, that outstanding conservative theologian, Dr. Benjamin B. Warfield of Princeton, maintained that in American Presbyterians no such action was necessary. It was not necessary, because the American Presbyterian Church for which the Bible was and continues to be "the only infallible rule of faith and practice" has committed its ministers only to the "system of doctrine" contained in the Confession. On several occasions throughout their history, American Presbyterian Churches have both modified their Subordinate Standards and supplemented with new articles the original text. This was done in full harmony with the spirit of the Reformed faith, and in obedience to the new light which the Holy Spirit shed upon the teaching of Holy Scripture. The same distinguished scholar and teacher just mentioned also held that the Reformed faith as a "system of doctrine" is equally contained in the Heidelberg Catechism, the Thirty-nine Articles of the Church of England and the Westminster Confession of Faith.

But who shall define this "system of doctrine"? The Church, of course, which adopted it and demands subscription to it, the Church which comes in lineal descent from the Commission of Presbyterian Churchmen who drafted the original document and approved it by majority vote. But in what capacity shall the Church have authority to do the defining? By a resolution of its General Assembly at any given time, or only by the direct vote of its constituent Presbyteries? This is no mere academic or theological question.

One of the bitterest conflicts in the history of American Presbyterianism centered around this very matter. In the twenties of the present century a General Assembly of the Presbyterian Church U.S.A. presumed it had the right to define the central tenets of the Christian faith, that is, the "system of doctrine" as contained in the historic Confession. More than a thousand Presbyterian ministers appended their signatures to a document called "The Auburn Affirmation." This document challenged the right of any given General Assembly to impose its judgment upon the whole Church on a matter affecting the Church's constitution. The majority of the signers did not take exception to the doctrines which had been specially singled out for emphasis. They affirmed, however, that the Assembly's procedure violated a basic principle in American Presbyterianism. This principle requires that only when the requisite number of Presbyteries vote favorably on a constitutional question is the General Assembly authorized to impose its collective will on fellow Presbyterians.

There followed a bitter decade of theological and ecclesiastical controversy. A small group of conscientious and ardent spirits, who were totally insensitive, however, to the soul of Presbyterianism in matters of Faith and Order, withdrew from the Church. For a time thereafter the discussion of theological questions was virtually banned, even by very conservative Presbyterians. They did not want more controversy.

In a few years, however, the cathartic had done its work. The Church received a new understanding of its heritage and mission. Theology was restored to its traditional place. The "Broadening Church" to use the designation of a distinguished Church historian, Dr. Lefferts A. Loetscher, who has dealt with this period of Presbyterian history, was on its way again, with a fresh vision of Truth and a deepened devotion to it.

We now pass on to deal concretely with the way in which Presbyterians interpret the three basic realities of the spiritual order—God, man, and the Church.

✠ **3** ✠

The Presbyterian
Understanding of God

To the ancient fool who said, "There is no God," and to his contemporary successor who says, "God is dead," Presbyterians join with Christians everywhere in a chant of faith, and say exultingly, in the words of the Apostles' Creed, "I believe in God the Father Almighty, Maker of Heaven and Earth."

The awe and bewilderment which have overtaken the human spirit with the advent of the Space Age has raised afresh for Christians and non-Christians alike the question of God and the cosmic order. The mystery of a pervasive orderliness which enables man to make impressive calculations, on the basis of which he launches missiles into outer space with astounding accuracy, has made it easy for reverent scientific minds to believe in God, at least as a cosmic principle of order. Let us listen to a spokesman for the New Age.

Taking as a text the words of the English poet, Alfred Noyes, "The universe is centered on neither the earth nor the sun—it is centered in God." A contemporary soldier scientist, John B. Medaris, recently made this statement: "In this busy age, in these days of intense scientific activity as we approach the conquest of space, it is not surprising that we find ourselves restless, unfulfilled, unsatisfied. Amidst all this kaleidoscopic movement, the inner soul of man must find an eternal harbor, some home port that will stay put, his own internal haven of peace. When he fails to find such an anchorage his mind refuses the challenge of change. Mental illness becomes an epidemic of the times, and youth, cast afloat on uncharted seas, lacks assurance. The cry of pain and insecurity rises from the hearts of the untrained—'Where am I?'—'Where am I going?' —'Who and where is the authority?' And the world is too busy to answer.

"Yet the answer is there. The answer is in the majestic order of the Universe and its obedience to unchanging law. This timeless, changeless order is an assurance of unchallenged authority, a sign of safe anchorage for the troubled spirit of man. Like the growth of a child from infant to adult, man is 'discovering' worlds new to him, but old to God.

"When this is fully realized man can stand straight and tall, assured in the face of apparent uncertainty, secure in the knowledge of the way home, at peace with himself because he is at peace with God."

But the God just described is not the Christian God. He is not the God who has inspired Presbyterians or given rise to any decisively Christian witness. Belief in a God who is above all else a Personal Principle of Order can give to the inquiring mind a certain sense of meaning. It can even create a feeling of at-homeness in the vast universe and give courage to the scientific spirit. But the restless, anguished soul of man needs more than a Deity who is a Super Mathematician, a Master Physicist, or even a Supreme Intelligence. Man craves to know God's character, to have a remedy for his experience of guilt, to find a haven for his storm-tossed spirit, to discover an answer to the problem of mankind and human history. In the background of the new Divinity of the Space Age and the timeless needs of man in every age, let us turn to the Christian understanding of God. I will deal very especially with those facets of God's Being and actions which have been particularly impressive to Presbyterians, have become part of their inmost being and have been portrayed by them in doctrine, sermon and song.

THE LIVING GOD

A sense of the majesty of God and His sovereign rule over nature and all things human has marked Presbyterian thought and life through the centuries. To this has been coupled in equal measure a sense of God's everlastingness and the brevity and transitoriness of the life of man. Sensitivity to these dimensions of reality have been due in no small measure to the use by Presbyterians of the Hebrew Psalms as a vehicle of praise in public and private worship. For generations the metrical version of the Psalms of David was the only medium of song permitted in Presbyterian circles in Geneva, Scotland and the United States. "Uninspired hymns" were excluded from the melodies sung in the sanctuary and around the family altar. Only the Spirit-inspired Book of Praise was permitted.

The criterion used to determine the proprieties of Christian worship may have been inexcusably narrow. It did mean, however, that the most matchless collection of religious poetry in all literature became an integral part of the Presbyterian heritage. The sublime sentiments of David and his peers regarding the Lord God of Israel, who was also the "God of the whole earth," entered into the soul of successive generations of Presbyterians, profoundly stirring their thought and imagination.

Listen to some of the refrains: "The Lord reigns; let the earth rejoice." "O, Lord how mighty is Thy name in all the earth." "The heavens are telling the glory of God; and the firmament proclaims His handiwork." "From everlasting to everlasting Thou art God." "My times are in Thy hand." "The Lord is the stronghold of my life; of whom shall I be afraid?" "Our days are but a handbreadth—teach me to number my days that I may get a heart of wisdom." "Trust in the Lord and do good, so you will dwell in the land and enjoy security."

"Blessed be the Lord God of Israel who alone does wondrous things." "Blessed be His glorious name forever, may His glory fill the wholo earth." No one from the days of Calvin to the living present could sing these rhapsodies without getting an overmastering sense of the living God. Here in moving melody are proclaimed God's majesty and sovereign sway. His gracious admission of man, the passing shadow to the shelter of His eternity, the security and significance of human life when related to God's purpose.

As one brought up on the Psalms, I can recall the thrill I once had in the philosophy classroom of Aberdeen University when I heard my Hegelian teacher, who usually took some unkind crack at Christian belief, say this: "In all human literature," said the translator of Hegel's *Phenomenology of Spirit*, "there is nothing that parallels the intimacy and directness of the conversation between God and man that is found in the Hebrew Psalms." This is profoundly true. In these ancient melodies there echoes a classical strain in the religion of the Bible which it has been given to Presbyterians to treasure, and to some degree to express in their historic witness. I refer to the union of a sense of God's greatness and transcendence with a sense of His gracious condescension in holding intercourse with the sinful transients of earth. To be able to say quietly to the Eternal God, the Ruler of earth and heaven, in a spirit of reverent awe and loving devotion, "Thou art my God forever and ever!"—Human life has no greater experience to offer than this. It should be observed, however, that in every instance there is an inseparable relation between the security which is the gift of God and the goodness which is the duty of man. In the Psalms as a whole, as in the Bible, there is no divine security for man that is not founded on human obedience to God.

GOD'S SOVEREIGN PURPOSE

God's infinite transcendence and boundless condescension are linked together in a sovereign eternal purpose. The Creator of all things has decreed the entire course of human history and has elected for Himself a covenant people. While the doctrine of the Divine Decree in Predestination and Election is by no means an exclusively Presbyterian doctrine, it has become closely associated with the Presbyterian name and with Presbyterian history. This particular doctrine has also been the subject of much controversy and misunderstanding. It is important, therefore, that it be considered at this time, and that its meaning, as understood by Presbyterians today, be made clear.

These momentous years offer an unusual setting for treating God's relationship to human life and history. The breakdown of familiar assumptions regarding progress, and the awareness that nuclear science confronts mankind with tragic possibilities, forces afresh upon contemporary thought the question as to whether there is a plan in the universe or whether Chance is King. Two other facts must also be borne in mind. The Communist powers, while they deny the existence of Deity, have a gay faith in the future of Humanity as represented by the world's Proletariat. This faith is grounded upon a philosophical affirmation regarding the presence in history of an inexorable on-going movement which will guarantee the victory of Communism. Democracy, on the other hand, especially American Democracy, is nervous and bewildered. It lacks the steadfast calm that springs from the assurance that God Almighty is working out His purposes in our time and that the future is with those whose chief concern is Righteousness rather than Security, who stand for moral integrity rather than political expediency.

In many respects the situation that confronts the world today is strangely analogous to the situation that confronted the Western World in Calvin's time. Calvin restored to thought the tremendous truth of God's Eternal Purpose whereby He controls human destiny and makes all historical happenings serve the welfare and triumph of His Chosen People, His Elect. Inasmuch as all things are in the hands of God, the main question for Calvin and his followers became, What is the revealed will of God? What is God's will for the Church? What is God's will for society? What is God's will for me?

It is clear that for Calvin, Knox and Witherspoon, and the dynamic leaders of Presbyterianism throughout the centuries, the doctrine of God's "Eternal Decree," whereby "God from all eternity did by the most wise and holy counsel of His own will freely and unchangeably ordain whatever comes to pass —and hath appointed the Elect unto glory—who are redeemed by Christ—and are effectually called unto faith by Christ by His Spirit working in due season," specially concerned believers in Christ who needed the assurance of their eternal salvation. It was designed also to inspire them with courage to stand for those things which they believed to be consonant with the will of God.

It is a significant fact in this connection that in his great work, *The Institutes of the Christian Religion,* Calvin discusses God's Eternal Decree in relation to his discussion of man, and not in the earlier section where he deals with God Himself, His nature and His attributes. Calvin's interest in Predestination was not to descant upon this august doctrine so replete with mystery, or to present it as a logical consequence of the nature of Deity. He deals with it rather as an explanation of God's redeeming grace in Christ and of the life of those who experienced the new life in Christ. They "were predestined unto Christ in good works before the foundation of the world and were in due course renewed by His spirit and united to His Son." In a word, Calvin was no cold scholastic logician, but a warm-hearted evangelical thinker. It is rather striking, moreover, that in the catechism which he wrote for the Church in Geneva the doctrine of the Eternal Decree, in which he believed so profoundly, does not appear at all.

As time passed, however, there came a period in Presbyterian thought when the Decrees of God were given a place of greater prominence than was the case in the theology of the early Reformers. By the time the Westminster Confession of Faith was written, we find the Doctrine of Divine Foreordination in a new perspective. Its formulation comes in logical sequence immediately after the Doctrine of the Trinity. It has often, moreover, given concern to Presbyterians that in that matchless little compendium of Christian truth, the Westminster Shorter Catechism, which was issued by the same Assembly that produced the historic Confession, the word "love" does not itself occur in the famous definition of God. The question, "What is God?" is answered thus—"God is a spirit, infinite, eternal and unchangeable in His being, wisdom, power holiness, justice, goodness and truth."

This famous definition was the symbol of a trend which manifested itself in circles that loved to glory in their orthodoxy and which set an idea about God above the Biblical reality of God as revealed in Christ. From an abstract concept of God and divine sovereignty they deduced by inexorable logic that God had predestined some men to damnation and others to salvation and that this division was equally applicable in the realm of childhood. Calvin, we know, as a result of a very bitter controversy, unfortunately allowed the cold logic of an idea about Deity to overcome the warm devotion to the God to whom he gave his heart in perfect trust. But his Presbyterian children in Scotland and America revolted against some unwarranted deductions from the doctrine of Predestination. This they did while thanking God for John Calvin, and in full loyalty to the Reformed faith as formulated by him, the genius of which, it should never be forgotten, is to go on reforming, in obedience to the fuller light which the Holy Spirit sheds upon the Word.

The concern of American Presbyterians led them to introduce the following statement into the Constitution of the new United Presbyterian Church:

"The United Presbyterian Church in the U.S.A. does authoritatively declare as follows: 1. "With reference to Chapter III of the Confession of Faith; that concerning those who are saved in Christ the Doctrine of God's Eternal Decree is held in harmony with the doctrine of His love to all mankind, His gift of His Son to be the propitiation for the sins of the whole world, and his readiness to bestow His saving grace on all who seek it; that concerning those who perish, the Doctrine of

God's eternal decree is held in harmony with the doctrine that God desires not the death of any sinner but has provided in Christ a salvation sufficient for all, adapted to all and freely offered in the Gospel to all; that men are fully responsible for their treatment of God's gracious offer; that his decree hinders no man from accepting that offer; and that no man is condemned except on the ground of his sin."

2. "With reference to Chapter X, Section 3 of the Confession of Faith, that it is not to be regarded as teaching that any who die in infancy are lost. We believe that all dying in infancy are included in the election of grace and are regenerated and saved by Christ who works when and where and how He pleases."

Several decades before the Church Union of 1958 took place, a sister Presbyterian church, commonly known as the "Southern Presbyterian Church," took similar action. This Church, noted for its theological conservatism and deep evangelical spirit, and which, incidentally, is one of the three largest Presbyterian Churches in the world, was authorized by its General Assembly to print a similar statement regarding "election" in the Church's edition of the Confession of Faith. While "A Brief Statement of Belief," the document in which the paragraph on "election" is included, has not been made a part of the Church's Constitution, its appearance as an Appendix to the Church's Confession is significant.

Two things stand out in high relief regarding the "Presbyterian Way" in our time. The first is this. As much as at any time in their history Presbyterians stand for the reality of God's eternal purpose in Christ for the world and for the certain triumph in history of the "Elect." The second thing is no less important. Presbyterians are equally agreed that no one who hears the Gospel is excluded from the benefits of the Gospel, save by his own decision. They affirm that no one can assign boundaries to the sovereign love of God or the operation of the Holy Spirit in making men participants in Christ's redemptive work. They also affirm that all who are incapable while in life of making normal human choices shall be incorporated by the Grace of Christ into that elect "Company which no man can number."

THE BOOK OF BOOKS

Presbyterians, however, while influenced by the Hebrew Psalms in their conception of God's majestic sovereignty and gracious nearness, have been students and lovers of the Scriptures as a whole in the best Protestant tradition. In the Constitution of the Presbyterian Church the authority of the Bible for Christian faith and behavior is proclaimed in the most unqualified way. The Old and New Testaments are cherished as the supreme and only authoritative record of God's self-disclosure to man for man's redemption. The Bible is above all else a book about Jesus Christ, God's Incarnate Son, who lived, died and rose again from the dead in order that men through faith in Him as their divine Saviour and Lord should be delivered from their sinful self-centeredness and become members of the People of God which is the Church, the Community of Christ. In an absolutely unique sense the Bible is the "Word of God,"—"the only infallible rule of faith and practice."

Upon the analogy of the Incarnation of Christ, the Bible is both human and divine. It, too, is found in the "Form of a Servant." It has traits which make clear that it was written by humans as a historic document which was in process of compilation for many centuries. In its texture are displayed very characteristic human features. Like the Christ who is its central theme, it belongs to history, while being at the same time history's greatest literary monument. The Bible can stand scrutiny in accordance with the severest canons of critical research. Recent archeological discoveries have given the Biblical records a new status as authentic history. The study of Biblical thought in terms of the categories that are native to the Book has established at a new level the incomparable development and unity of its message. Starting from the reality of Revelation which is the Bible's basic category, it has become clear to thoughtful and devout Presbyterian men and women who are passionately devoted to the Scriptures and to Christ, that the supreme authority of the Bible in all matters relating to faith and life has nothing whatever to do with the verbal inerrancy of the Biblical text. It has become equally clear, by objective evidence, that a person may affirm that he "believes the Bible from cover to cover," without giving the slightest evidence that he takes the message of the Bible seriously, or that he manifests the mind of Christ in his personal attitudes and behavior. Spiritually he may be a perfect pagan.

For Presbyterians, as for other Christians in our time, there has dawned a great new era of intelligent enthusiasm for the Bible and of faith in the Bible as distinguished from an unbiblical and demoralizing bibliolatry. It has been brought home to them that only in one way can the Bible be creatively studied. When the reader comes to the Book of Books seeking an answer to the deepest questions regarding his life in relation to God and man, he will come face to face with the God-man. He will be confronted with life's supreme decision to "believe in the name of the Son of God." It is also coming home to Presbyterians and to others that only in the measure in which the Holy Spirit, who is the ultimate author of the Biblical revelation, creates an inward response in the soul of him who seeks to know the Biblical truth, will rapport be established between the reader and the Book. The human heart must respond "Thou art my God, my Saviour, my Lord."

It will be helpful, if I conclude this brief discussion of the Bible as the supreme source of our knowledge of God by transcribing some paragraphs from the Westminster Study Bible. This outstanding volume, issued in 1946 by the Board of Christian Education of the Presbyterian Church in the U.S.A., was a pioneer in these last times in promoting the intelligent study of the Bible among American Christians. From the introductory chapter entitled "God Has Spoken" I quote these words: "What is the Bible essentially? It is the record of God's revelation to mankind, the abiding witness to the fact that he has spoken. *God Has Spoken.* This is the message of the Bible. There is a word from the Lord which makes known the very heart and mind of God in relation to the world and to man. Light has shone upon the mystery of man's life, a divine answer has been given to the problem of his sin. The hidden God has become manifest in redemptive activity, designed to recreate the life of mankind. The one stupendous fact with which the Bible deals is that God has spoken by saving deeds and enlightening words. The Book is the record of his self-communication at different times and through diverse agents. It is thereby in a wholly unique sense, the "Word of God."

Here is what has been classically described in the Presbyterian heritage of faith as "The Eternal and Inviolable Truth." This is the Book which has been restored to theological significance in our time by Karl Barth, that contemporary disciple of Calvin, who has unashamedly made the Bible and the Bible alone the basis for his massive structure of theological thought.

GOD IN THREE PERSONS

God is revealed in the Bible as a Trinity, Father, Son and Holy Spirit. With the Universal Christian Church, Presbyterians have always been and continue to be Trinitarian in their faith regarding Deity. Their faith is monistic in that it affirms that there is but one God; it is Trinitarian in affirming that there are three Persons in the Godhead, each of whom has fulfilled, and continues to fulfill a specific role in carrying out God's eternal purpose for mankind.

My first memory of Christian doctrine goes back to the earliest years of my boyhood. The minister of the church to which my parents belonged was a doctrinal preacher in the great tradition of Highland Scotch Presbyterianism. Time and again at a Sabbath service there would fall upon my ears this refrain "All things are *of* the Father; all things are *through* the Son; all things are *by* the Spirit." The truth could not fail to sink into my boyish mind that the three Persons of the Trinity are not members in a static reality. The Holy Three, who in the words of the Westminster Shorter Catechism are "One God, the same in substance, equal in power and glory," existed in a dynamic, vocational relationship to one another and to mankind. This early introduction to theology was a good preparation for accepting without difficulty the famous and controversial "filioque," that the Holy Spirit flows from the Son as well as from the Father. It helped me also to maintain in manhood years that the Christian God, who is revealed in three Persons, is missionary by His very nature.

THE FATHER ALMIGHTY

The Father Almighty of the great Christian Creeds is the creative source and the providential sustainer of all things that exist, visible and invisible. He is the Covenant God of Abraham, Isaac and Jacob, and the Lord God of Israel, His Servant. He is the God and Father who gave His Son Jesus Christ to be the Saviour of the world and to reconcile all things to Himself.

Nowhere in the Christian ages is the Fatherhood of God and the tenderness of His love so movingly and luminously portrayed as in Rembrandt's painting of the "Return of the Prodigal Son." The whole picture is swathed in that strange metaphysical light for which the art of Rembrandt is famous. No fingers were ever drawn of mortal man to match those on the Father's hands that touch the penitent young vagabond just returned from the "far country." The nature of the spiritual world and the inmost heart of Deity stand revealed.

Rembrandt was a Dutchman, reared in the Calvinistic Reformed Church of his native land. In his paintings he succeeded in interpreting that rediscovery of the infinite love of God which came with the Protestant Reformation. The following words of a great art critic, G. Baldwin Brown, are important in this connection: "Rembrandt was the first painter to convey through his design the spirit of Protestant Christianity in its most enlightened form." Referring to Rembrandt's "Return of the Prodigal Son," the same writer says,

"Rembrandt entered more deeply into the Pauline theology and conceived of the Divine Fatherhood, incorporating itself in the infinite compassion, the all-embracing tenderness of Christ. This is the significance of the great religious picture, the last painting from his hand. There is here embodied in the moving presentment of the return of the prodigal to the father, whose compassion fails not, the doctrine of the relation between the divine and mortal that can best be expressed in the terms of human fatherhood."

It is a moving fact that, soon after painting this picture, Rembrandt died. He passed away as a social prodigal, "an undischarged bankrupt, who had nothing to call his own but his clothes and his painting materials." Only those who have wandered far and lost everything can truly appreciate the love and forgiveness of the Eternal Father.

"HIS ONLY SON OUR LORD"

When Presbyterians repeat together the words of the Apostles' Creed, affirming their belief "in Jesus Christ His only Son our Lord," they join again in the chorus of faith of Christ's Church Universal. In their Confession and Catechisms they add their own refrain to the classical affirmations regarding Jesus Christ which are found in the great creeds of Christendom. The doctrines of the Virgin Birth of the God-man, of his true but sinless manhood, his vicarious Death upon the cross, his glorious Resurrection, and his Ascension to the seat of celestial power, where He continues to fulfill the functions of his mediatorial office and to exercise kingly rule, and from which He will come again for the redemption of his people and the judgment of the world, are all parts of Presbyterian theology.

Very real also in the faith and life of Presbyterians has been the doctrine of the three-fold office of Christ as Prophet, Priest and King. "Christ as our Redeemer," says the Westminster Shorter Catechism, "executeth the office of a prophet, of a priest, and of a king, both in His estate of humiliation and exaltation." Moving and simple, yet profound and relevant to life in its wholeness, is the description of the three offices. "Christ executeth the office of a prophet in revealing to us by His Word and Spirit, the Will of God for our Salvation." He "executeth the office of a priest in his once offering up of Himself, a sacrifice to satisfy divine justice and reconcile us to God, and in making continual intercession for us." He "executeth the office of a king in subduing us to Himself, in ruling and defending us, and in restraining and conquering all His and our enemies."

Both in their theological heritage and their historical witness, Presbyterians have been profoundly Christocentric. The Son of God, who is central in the Godhead and in God's unfolding purpose, has been dynamically central in their doctrine and their experience. In many a historical struggle in Church and Society in which Presbyterians have been engaged Christ has been "Lord of all." Differences of opinion there have been. Even bitter controversies have raged regarding the theological theory that most adequately interprets this or that cardinal, and passionately accepted event, in the redemption which Jesus Christ wrought. But when Presbyterians have been true to themselves and to their heritage of faith they have always been able to distinguish between absolute faith in a great Christian event, and their all-too-human way of interpreting that event. Time and again, as Scottish Church history shows, immense sacrifices were made in defense of the "Crown Rights of the Redeemer," who was the "sole Head of the Church" and the ultimate "King of Scotland."

References abound in Presbyterian history and biography to an intense sense of the Real Presence of Christ. From a book entitled "The Evangelical Movement in the Highlands of Scotland," by John MacInnes, published by the Aberdeen University Press in 1951, I take this paragraph: "The consciousness of the real presence of the Saviour was intense in the great congregations which gathered to the Highland sacraments. Of the Kiltearn communion of 1785 it was said, 'There was an extraordinary manifestation of the Saviour's gracious presence in the congregation. When the service concluded

many of the Lord's people from their ecstasy of soul and joy
of spirit, did not know whether they were in the body or out
of the body!' "

But I hear the question being asked, "Is there one facet of
the person and work of Christ which could be regarded as
being in a very special sense a Presbyterian emphasis, beyond
the acknowledged emphasis upon the 'Lordship of Christ'?"
My answer would be this: A true understanding of the mediatorial work of Jesus Christ as the "one mediator between God
and man," in His life, death and resurrection, and the abiding
implication of this understanding for Christian thought and
life, has been a special Presbyterian concern. I also believe
that in this realm the Reformed and Presbyterian tradition has
made, and continues to make, a very decided contribution to
the Church Universal.

The painter Rembrandt, as I have already remarked, was a
Dutch Calvinist. A French writer, Wencelius, has written a
book entitled *Calvin and Rembrandt*. He presents the thesis
that Rembrandt is the only painter who, in his portrayal of
episodes from the life of Christ, really succeeds in doing justice
to both his divinity and his humanity. Christ as the Man-God
appears in Rembrandt's art in no static pose but in action. To
those who accompanied Him He mediated the reality of His
divine nature. Christ's mediation of His Godhead in a sublime manner is pictorially represented in Rembrandt's canvas
of the Supper scene at the close of the journey to Emmaus.
A strange metaphysical light shines in the face of the Guest
who becomes Host. Wencelius reinforces his viewpoint by
quoting a passage from an art critic, Valentiner, who in the preface to his book, *Collection of Art Classics*, writes thus: "He
(Rembrandt) has been not only the greatest but the only
painter of Jesus. The Italians have made of Jesus a young God.
The Germans have made of Him a man often vulgar and ugly.
Rembrandt alone has had the vision of the Man-God, a soul in
converse with misery, but turned towards eternity. Beneath
an unlikely covering God is revealed." The great Dutch painter
presents Jesus Christ in a way that transmits a special insight

and emphasis of the Christian tradition to which he himself belonged.

Let me give another illustration of Presbyterian concern for the honor and rights of the "one mediator between God and man." During the past decade Presbyterians became deeply stirred on account of the new status that has been given progressively by the Roman Catholic Church to the Virgin Mary as the supreme mediatrix between God and the soul, and between God and the course of history. The General Assembly of 1955 of the Presbyterian Church U.S.A. approved a document entitled "The Lordship of Christ in relation to the Marian Cult," which a previous Assembly had asked a special committee to prepare. In this basic study of the most recent developments in the realm of Mariolatry we read, "As for churches in the Protestant tradition, they affirm, now as ever, the exclusive and sovereign Kingship of Jesus Christ in the Church, and the sufficiency of His mediatorial work for men. The same Christ who in Biblical language sits 'at the right hand of God' is the sovereign Lord of history. He is also everlastingly accessible to the cry of human need. He still reveals himself to men in a saving encounter. He indwells each Christian soul that is open to His abiding presence. He is the Road Companion of every Christian who lives to make Him known to men as the Light and Life of mankind and who takes seriously His promise—'Lo, I am with you always, even unto the end of the world.'"

The Marian Cult, the document went on to emphasize, constitutes a challenge to Presbyterians and to all Christians, Roman and non-Roman alike. "The glory of Christ's lordship in His Church, His undying concern for the members of His Body and for all human beings, is both tarnished and challenged by the new status accorded to the Virgin. The meaning of Christ's Kingship for life and history becomes emptied of all true significance. What is more serious still, the Holy Spirit recedes into the background and the Virgin becomes virtually the paraclete, the Holy Ghost incarnate." Here is a contemporary echo of a concern for the unique Kingship and continuous mediatorial status of Christ, in the Church and in the world, that has marked Presbyterianism from its earliest days to the present.

"THE HOLY GHOST, THE LORD AND GIVER OF LIFE"

Calvin, it has been said, was in a supreme sense "the theologian of the Holy Spirit." In creation and in redemption all things have been *by* the Spirit. The Spirit brooded over chaos and brought a cosmos into being. The Spirit directed the course of Israel's history and inspired the writers of the Bible. To the power of the Spirit was due the Incarnation of Christ and the equipment of the God-man for his redemptive work. Through the Eternal Spirit Christ offered Himself up without spot unto God. By the same power of the Spirit, He rose again from the dead. The Spirit "who proceedeth from the Father and the Son" descended upon the infant Church at Pentecost. It is by the inward work of the Spirit that sinful men are regenerated and conformed to the likeness of Christ. It is by the testimony of the Holy Spirit that the human spirit is led to recognize the Word of God in Holy Scripture. The proclamation of the Gospel is made effective in the salvation of men by the accompanying power of the Spirit. By the light of the Spirit the Christian Church is guided into all truth. Under the Spirit's guidance new insights into God's Revelation are being constantly given to the Spirit-filled soul.

There is a sense, however, in which, following the glow of the Reformation period, the full Biblical dimension of the work of the Holy Spirit tended to pass out of the Presbyterian consciousness, as indeed it faded in its fullness from the consciousness of most Christian Churches. It was not that belief in the Third Person of the Trinity declined. The doctrine of the Spirit continued to form an essential part of Protestant orthodoxy, especially as the Inspirer of the Scriptures and the Regenerator and Sanctifier of the Christian soul. What tended to become lost was a due sense of the abiding presence of the Holy Spirit in the Church. The multiple fractions into which Protestantism in general, and Protestant denominations in particular, became divided, was not conducive to the prevalence in the Church of a high doctrine of the abiding reality of the Spirit of truth and love. Theological and ecclesiastical structures became frozen. In Presbyterian circles the subtle, implicit assumption prevailed that, so far as theological truth was concerned, the Holy Spirit had done his work and had already led the Church into all truth.

Strangely, paradoxically, the original Westminster Confession of Faith contained no specific article on the Holy Spirit. In American Presbyterianism this deficiency began to be repaired at the beginning of the present century. An article on "The Holy Spirit" was added to the historic Confession together with another article on "the Gospel of the love of God and Missions." Very appropriate in this connection is an observation made by Professor George H. Hendry of Princeton Theological Seminary. In a book recently issued by the John Knox Press, Richmond, Virginia, Dr. Hendry says, "If it be true that the Holy Spirit points to the creativity, the freedom, and the inwardness of the work of God, it could be said that the Westminster Confession of Faith reflects a type of theology which tends to stabilize the relations between God and man within the framework of a rigid system, in which the freedom of God Himself is circumscribed and which makes it difficult to distinguish the inwardness of faith from intellectual acceptance of a doctrinal system. A Confession of Faith which contains a chapter on the Holy Spirit is reminded of the limited scope and function of all doctrinal formulations, which can point toward the gospel but can never contain it."

Happily, in these last years, a sense of the living reality of the Holy Spirit has been growing in Presbyterian and other Christian Churches. The issues inherent in our revolutionary time, this ecumenical, atomic, space era, the awareness of the futility of human wisdom in guiding the destinies of the Church in the achievement of unity and the fulfillment of mission, a rediscovery of the full dimension of the Biblical outlook on the Holy Spirit, and above all the challenge and lessons of the Pentecostal Movement around the world, have put new meaning for Presbyterians and all fellow Christians into the great affirmation, "I believe in the Holy Ghost, the Lord and Giver of life."

THE GOSPEL OF GOD

This chapter is already long, but a basic question still remains. What is the central involvement of the Holy Trinity, and how do Presbyterians interpret it?

The dynamic unity of the Godhead and, if I may be allowed to say it in reverent, though very human terms, the missionary role of each Person in the Holy Trinity are expressed in a special manner in the Gospel. The Gospel of God, the Gospel of Christ, is the central theme of the Bible and of Christian religion when true to itself.

What is the Gospel? Let me answer this question in my Presbyterian way by trying to interpret the loyalty which is deepest in the Presbyterian soul and most central in the Presbyterian heritage of faith.

What is the "Good News" which lies at the heart of the "Evangel" of the "Gospel"? It is "Good News" about God.

If I say "God exists," that is good news. For if there is a Supreme Being, then life has a meaning, history has a goal, man has a Master. A famous Scotsman, afterwards familiarly known as Rabbi Duncan, did a dance on the old Brig of Dee, in Aberdeen, when, as a young agnostic he could believe with intellectual honesty in the existence of Deity.

But the mere theistic affirmation is not the Gospel. Merely to be religious is not to be evangelical. Religion is not necessarily a good thing. Religious people are not inevitably good people. Everything depends on the religion a man has, and the God in whom he believes. It was Pascal who said, "Men never do evil so heartily as when they do it from religious conviction." History's annals are stained by unspeakable atrocities committed in the name of God and religion.

If I say "God is love," that is good news; that is indeed better news. For if God is love, He is concerned, He cares about people. If He is love He is no snobbish Olympian Potentate, aloof in his detachment; nor yet a celestial summer Tourist on the roads of earth. If God is love He is not a cosmic Playwright who has staged in history a tragic drama for His entertainment. If God is love then the ultimate values are not dialectical or aesthetic, but personal.

But merely to say "God is love" is not to proclaim the Gospel. For this affirmation regarding the native benignancy of God's nature leaves totally unanswered some of life's major questions. Is the love of God love for good people, people who by their character qualify to be loved? "Can God possibly love me with my terrible record?" says an anguished spirit. "If He does, is there anything He can do about it? May He not be finite and impotent when confronted with the inexorable structure of the Universe? Until that question is answered, my spirit's need is unfilled, its anxiety unmet."

The Christian Gospel is something that goes far beyond Theism and Idealism. It is the joyous proclamation that God *did* something that He *became* something to show His love. It is the glad announcement that Deity became involved in human existence, that the Almighty got into the grim game of life. The best loved and most classical words in which the Gospel is proclaimed are sounded in St. John's Gospel: "For God so loved the world that He gave His only begotten Son, that whoever believes in Him should not perish, but have eternal life." Here, in this best-known and loved of all verses in the Bible, are the two essential aspects of the Christian "Good News." First, what God did *for* man; and second, what God can do *in* man.

What did God do *for* man? He *became* man. The God-man, Jesus Christ, who had "a true body and a reasonable soul" fought man's battle with temptation. He was not a phantom man. He *stood* where the original man *succumbed* to the Tempter. Confronted with three basic issues relating to His task as the Saviour of men, He stood fast. In an hour of crisis He refused to make the satisfaction of physical need the ultimate motive of human behavior. He refused to validate his messianic claims by a spectacular publicity stunt. He refused to conquer the world by subjecting Himself in ultimate loyalty to the hard facts about man and society, an attitude commonly regarded as essential for all who would achieve worldly power. He rejected the Prince of this world.

The "Son of God the Saviour" took the "Way of the Cross." Having already won a victory for man over the Deceiver of men, he restored and made visible in His life the lost image of man. "Behold the man!" How Jesus' eyes blazed with fury and his hands grasped a lash when people were being exploited and religion was being degraded in the House of His Father! How the same eyes shed tears of compassion in the presence of sorrowful people or over a beloved city headed for doom! How his hands fondled and blessed children, and with loving gesture he healed the sick and raised the dead! Taking the "Way of the Cross" Jesus Christ crossed out the sins of men. Abandoned by His friends, accused by the representatives of history's purest religion, booed by the fickle masses that had acclaimed him Israel's King, knowingly condemned to death as an innocent man by the representative of a power that gloried in its justice, abused in dying by the soldiers of a mighty empire, the Son of Man triumphed over men. And at the last He made man's lost image visible when, moments before the end, he said from the Cross, "Father, forgive them for they know not what they do." The Saviour of the world had won his right to die by showing Himself a true man, a sinless man, the representative of man. The Good News that Jesus Christ qualified to die a vicarious death is a very essential part, and an all too forgotten part, of the Christian Gospel. It is a phase which Presbyterians deeply cherish.

Upon the cross Jesus Christ, God's Eternal Son, died for the sins of the whole world. In Christ Crucified the infinite forgiving love of God became manifest in a supreme sacrificial act to reconcile the world to Himself. No human theory of the Atonement can adequately explain the august mystery of all that happened at Calvary during the hours of the Crucifixion. The Crucified shouted, "It is finished." "The third day He rose again from the dead." "He ascended into heaven and sitteth at the right hand of God the Father Almighty." He is accessible to every soul that seeks Him. He founded and became the head of His Body the Church, sending forth the Holy Spirit to be in it for ever. All these events and acts are part of the Glad Tidings of the Gospel.

And then there is the subjective phase of the Good News. What does God do *in* man, upon the basis of faith in the Crucified and Risen Christ, and through the operation of the Holy Spirit in the heart? Men are born again; their sins are forgiven; they have peace with God; they are united to Christ and to one another; they are made partakers of everlasting life and are given strength to overcome the world. The reality of inward change and the new life in Christ are also part of the same Gospel. This will receive fuller treatment in the next chapter when we come to deal with the doctrine of man.

In the meantime, let me close this chapter with some sentences from the new article on the "Gospel of the Love of God and Missions" which American Presbyterians added to their Confession of Faith. "God in infinite and perfect love, having provided in the Covenant of Grace through the mediation and sacrifice of the Lord Jesus Christ, a way of life and salvation, sufficient for and adapted to the whole lost race of man, doth freely offer this salvation to all men in the Gospel."

✤ 4 ✤

The Presbyterian
Understanding of Man

W<small>HAT</small> is man? The question about man, the so-called an-
thropological question, is the most crucial question of our time.
It is crucial for both Democracy and Communism. In this
revolutionary era when the world witnesses a new Revolt of
Man, the emergence of flaming nationalisms and the formation
of new states, people are forced to ask, what constitutes a real
human being? When is man truly man? What is the destiny of
man and how can he fulfill it?

In the Western World there have emerged a new philosophy
and a new psychology of man. Neither has any use for traditional religion. Both tend however to become religious as they
undertake to deal with the basic human issue.

The new philosophy is called Existentialism. Denying the
existence of God and the reality of an essence in man, this
philosophy proclaims the importance of man. Man in all his
brokenness and solitariness must assume full responsibility for
himself and for the world. Existentialism is the first philosophy
in the history of thought that starts from man's inner moods
and moves out from there to interpret the meaning of life and
to construct a true human existence.

The new psychology is Psychoanalysis. It is interested in man coming to know himself in order that he may be able to save himself. Psychoanalysis, which, in its vocational manifestation, is called Psychiatry, has virtually become a new religion whose God is the Analytical.

We also witness in our time an intense effort to recover the reality of man as an individual person. Amid the impersonality of mass society, the drift and the welter, the anxiety and the meaninglessness of contemporary life, the human individual has become lost. Representative and symbolical are such books as *Man Against Humanity, The Outsider* and *Organization Man.*

This context becomes part of the wider context of Holy Scripture and human history, of Christian doctrine and Presbyterian theology, as we now seek to interpret and set in due perspective the Presbyterian understanding of man. As in the previous chapter, in dealing with the subject of God, we become acutely aware of the fact that Christian theology was never more important than it is today. Such is the contemporary situation that it becomes imperative for all Christians to share with one another their deepest insights into the central realities of the common faith.

THE IMAGE OF GOD IN MAN

"God created man, male and female, after his own image, in knowledge, righteousness, and holiness, with dominion over the creatures." So runs the answer in the Westminster Shorter Catechism to the question, "How did God create man?"

For Presbyterians, as for other Christians in the great classical tradition of the faith, man is God's creation. "God created man in his own image" are the words of the Biblical account of creation. As to the precise manner or process of man's creation, that is a question for science to explore. What concerns Christian faith is the fact of man's divine origin, not the how of his historical development. Faith also affirms that man was made *like* God, that the image of God, or God-likeness, constitutes man's essence, that is, the core of human nature. It equally affirms that true manhood and the fulfillment of human destiny are inseparable from the manifestation of God-likeness in the life of man.

Very luminous and apposite are the words in which the Shorter Catechism answers the tremendous question "What is the chief end of man?" What is man *for* in this world? When can it be said that he is living at his truest and best, that he is fulfilling his human vocation?

Here is the famous answer which has stirred Presbyterian souls through the generations: "Man's chief end is to glorify God and to enjoy Him forever." To be a true man, to give expression to the inmost essence of human nature, to fulfill one's destiny, is to "glorify God." To "glorify" is a Biblical word which means to "unveil the splendor." For a man to "glorify God" is to make manifest in his own personality and behavior the character of God. He at the same time fits his life into God's great scheme of things, so that God can carry out his purposes through him. A human personality is truest to himself when he is most loyal to God. Then he "enjoys" God. It is when we lose ourselves in self-forgetfulness by our obedience to God that we find ourselves again in holy, rapturous communion with God. Here is a mystic note which is native to Presbyterian experience at its best. To "enjoy God" is something very different from "enjoying" a religious service, or a sermon, or a book of Christian devotion. To "enjoy God" in this sense means to "walk with God" in holy companionship on the road of Christian obedience, with eyes set upon the goal of human existence, the coming of God's Kingdom. It is to walk to the strains of this inward melody: "Thy Kingdom come, Thy will be done on earth, as it is done in Heaven." It is to devote one's life to the concerns of the Kingdom.

Man does not exist for his own sake, but for God's sake. A true man is God's man, a man who becomes a medium, a servant, whereby God manifests Himself and carries out His purpose.

The image of God in man is not to be regarded as a static

reflection of the Being of God; it is rather a dynamic likeness which manifests itself in active response to the Will of God and the Word of God. It entails, as Calvin puts it, not merely a knowledge that God is, but a perception of His will toward us. Thomas F. Torrance, a leading Reformed theologian of our time who is Professor of Theology at the University of Edinburgh, stresses in his work this dynamic character of the image of God in man. This image becomes manifest, he says, only in terms of man's knowledge of God, his continuous conformity to God, and his obedience to God and to God's claim upon him.

When, therefore, does man truly exist? The answer is this. Man truly exists when in his life and behavior he reflects the image of God, that likeness to God which man had and lost, and which was restored in Jesus Christ. Man does not truly exist by mere self-conscious activity. It is not true to say, with one great thinker, "I think, therefore I am," nor with another, "I struggle, therefore I am." Man exists when he can say with his whole being "I know Him, God in Jesus Christ, I give myself to Him, I obey Him, I serve Him."

But man, as we currently know him, and as the Existentialist describes him, is not this kind of a man. He is a being with a "holy emptiness, a noumenal hunger," full of a deep anguish and anxiety. It is no sufficient answer to recommend to him that for authentic living he must just accept his fatalistic lot with undaunted courage, his guilt included. For Presbyterians, as for all evangelical Christians, the human situation is different. They are quite as realistic as is the Existentialist about man's sense of guilt, and his feeling of emptiness, hunger and anxiety. But they go on to say: Man is a sinner. He was made by God for Himself, but he proclaims his independence and wants to be on his own. Yet his human heart is restless and will continue to be so, until it finds its rest in God. Man needs wholeness, health, salvation; his whole nature needs renewal, rebirth. First however there must break into his mind a light that comes from God. Before man's situation can change and he enter upon a new state of being, he must in the light of God come to know the truth about himself as he is, as he should be, and as he may become. In God's light, and in God's light alone, can man understand himself and the possibilities of his existence.

This brings us to consider man as he is, man in chains, a prisoner of his own iron will.

MEN IN CHAINS

We recall that famous dictum of Rousseau, "Man was born free, but everywhere he is in chains." This French writer, by his extreme doctrine of the freedom and innate goodness of human nature, prepared the way for a new tyranny. Christian faith, on the other hand, started from the recognition that there is in human nature a native tendency toward evil, which is called original sin, and provided for the realization of human freedom in the fullest degree.

Man as we know him is a sinner. It has been a characteristic of Presbyterian thought to emphasize with the utmost realism the sinfulness of man's nature, both as regards the waywardness of his behavior and the inward corruption of his whole being. This does not mean that there are no vestiges of goodness in the "natural man," or that no traces of the Creator's image are visible in his character. It does mean, however, that man, both in thought and action, is entirely off-center. He rejects the true goal of his existence which is to love and obey God. He makes *himself* the object of his devotion. Whether he consciously believes it, or vocally expresses it, the whole spirit of man inspires this melody, "Glory to man in the Highest." No one ever loved people as Jesus Christ did. Yet it is clear from the Gospel narrative that in His view of man Jesus was a realist, and that he had no illusions regarding human nature. "He knew what was in man," we are told.

Presbyterians have always emphasized and continue to emphasize today the two phases of human sin, one the negative the other positive. The negative phase is classically formulated in the Shorter Catechism. The question "What is sin?" is answered thus, "Sin is any want of conformity unto, or transgression of the law of God." To sin is, therefore, to fall short of the divine standard for human behavior. This standard Jesus Christ formulated in these words, "to love God with all one's heart, soul, strength and mind and to love one's neighbor as oneself." This true objective law of man's life, the love of God and neighbor, man "falls short of." He fails, by "want of conformity," to manifest this kind of love. Or else he goes beyond this standard, that is, he transgresses the divine law by running counter to it, thereby obeying some other law.

What is this substitute law? That great Christian churchman, St. Augustine, Bishop of Hippo, who profoundly influenced John Calvin and the whole Reformed tradition, considered that the deepest thing in human nature, as we know it, is concupiscence, which means ardent, lustful desire. To concupiscence, Augustine attributes the Fall of Man at the beginning. And we well know, of course, that in his famous *Confessions,* he speaks of the lustful passion that was his own master, that held him "in chains" for eleven long years, until in a garden in Milan the words came to him with liberating power, "Put on the Lord Jesus Christ and make no provision for the flesh to gratify its desires."

Profounder, however, was the insight of Calvin in regarding pride, not concupiscence, as the cause of man's fall, as well as the overmastering force in fallen human nature. The first man wanted to be "like God," to become a little God in his own right. Man's great sin through the ages to this day has been the pretension to be God's rival. He has interpreted "God-likeness" to mean not the manifestation of perfect self-giving love, but rather as self-centeredness, whereby a man makes his personal interests the exclusive or supreme object of his concern.

The poet, John Milton, true son of Calvin in poetry as Rembrandt was in art, makes pride the secret of the fall of Satan. In his great epic poem, *Paradise Lost,* one of the glories of world literature, Milton puts these words into the mouth of the fallen Archangel, who "trusted to have equalled the most High."

"O sun, to tell thee how I hate thy beams,
That bring to my remembrance from what state
I fell, how glorious once above thy sphere
Till pride and worse ambition threw me down,
Warring in Heaven against Heaven's matchless King.

Much has been spoken in these last times about the Demonic. What is the Demonic? The Demonic is the pretension of anything that is purely finite to take the place of the infinite, together with the ruthless spirit and fateful consequences that accompany this pretension. The Demonic appears when a nation or a race, a clan or a single individual, assumes the attributes of Deity, and in doing so, unlike true Deity, becomes absolutely self-centered. Just as the essence of human goodness is to be God-centered, so the essence of human sin is to be self-centered. Proud self-centeredness leads by inexorable stages to the moment when there takes place in the life of a human spirit or group a transvaluation of all values, an enthrallment to evil, the adoption of a new law of life and standard of living. This total moral collapse is symbolized by these words of Milton's Satan: "Farewell remorse! All good to me is lost. Evil be thou my good."

Earlier in the present century the dread reality of the Demonic manifested itself chiefly in the elevation of some collective reality into the place of absolute devotion. In Communist societies and in extreme forms of Nationalism this still continues. In democratic society today, and very especially in our American society, the problem of the Demonic is different. The affirmation of the right of uninhibited individual freedom, freedom to be fully one's self, to do whatever one takes into one's head to do; to violate any conventional standard or ethical sanctity, if only one succeeds in achieving one's desire, is regarded in many circles as man's birthright and the evidence of human maturity. This is the great new freedom. But freedom for what? It is, strangely enough, freedom to fulfill that concept of freedom which has been the bane and tragedy of the Hispanic World. This is the traditional freedom in which a people gloried who never developed a sense of sin, the freedom which is enshrined in the annals that recount the Spanish conquest of the Western World. It is expressed in a famous adage: "This Castilian is authorized to do whatever he takes into his head to do." Anarchic freedom has always been the prelude to dictatorship. It will be so again.

The "American way of life," which is so much lauded today in church and secular circles in our nation, is deeply infected with this negative anarchic conception of freedom, a conception so utterly alien to the true American tradition. The refusal to submit to absolute standards of behavior, the canonization of desire, and the enthronement of self-interest and personal advancement into the seat of Deity, constitute a new serfdom. Personal popularity, favorable public opinion, the acclaim of the masses, the satisfaction of appetites, the increase of dividends, the lure of political office, the attainment of national grandeur, the achievement of ballistic power, all in the sunshine of security—"These be Thy Gods, O Israel." When these goals are pursued as absolutes, as they are in innumerable instances, they become sacred divinities in the Pantheon of a new and ominous national spirit. Their worshipers, though they know it not, are "men in chains," bound by the "chains of their own iron wills." Glorying in their freedom, they are the abject slaves of their willful determination to follow the cravings of desire or the dictates of pride which have become their masters.

The Puritans, in the words of a Harvard historian, "refused to glorify the natural man." They refused because they knew that the natural man, despite his airs and illusions, is a slave. He needs to be set free. What true human freedom means, how it is to be achieved and where Presbyterians stand with regard to it will engage our thought in the next section.

GOD'S FREE MEN

It is one of the paradoxes of human life that man experiences the exhilaration of freedom as a positive, creative force when he gives himself up with all that he is and has, to something bigger than himself, that seems worthy of his supreme devotion. That something may be an idea, a cause, or a person. The quality of the "free" life will depend, of course, upon the object of devotion. But in every instance the person who is loyally obedient to some objective reality, whatever that reality may be, is a much more potent being than the person whose action is determined by a purely subjective impulse or selfish concern. This is the reason why Communists today can be such formidable people, while so many citizens of democratic countries who have developed a purely negative view of freedom, are such feeble folk.

Only when man gives himself unreservedly to God does he become free in the fullest sense. Only then can he achieve the solution of the whole complex of problems that are inherent in his nature as a sinful being. For true freedom is complete conformity to the Absolute.

Christian freedom is impressively described in a great hymn written by a Scottish Presbyterian minister, George Matheson. Let me quote two stanzas:

"Make me a captive, Lord.
And then I shall be free:
Force me to render up my sword,
And I shall conqueror be.
My will is not my own
Till Thou hast made it thine:
If it would reach a monarch's throne
It must its crown resign."

The process whereby a self-centered sinner in whose spirit a sense of guilt has developed, who has become aware of his human frailty, and sincerely desires to be a new person and to enter upon a life of freedom, is described in that loved compendium of Presbyterian theology, *The Westminster Shorter Catechism*. Liberation from the bondage of sinful self-centeredness depends on two things, Faith and Repentance. Re-echoing two of the central notes of the New Testament and of Evangelical Christianity, the Catechism thus defines the faith that saves, "Faith in Jesus Christ is a saving grace, whereby we receive and rest upon Him alone for salvation, as he is offered to us in the Gospel." This outward apprehension of Christ and commitment to Him is accompanied by an inward repentance, "metanoia." A total change is effected in the spirit and direction of a person's life involving the due renunciation of his old way of living. "Repentance unto life," we read, "is a saving grace, whereby a sinner out of a true sense of his sin, and apprehension of the mercy of God in Christ, doth with grief and hatred of his sin, turns from it unto God, with full purpose of and endeavor after new obedience."

This great spiritual change, by which a "servant of sin" becomes in a new sense a child of God and is adopted into the family of God, is a fruit of the inward working of the Holy Spirit. It is accompanied by two great events, one an act of God, the other a work of God. In the language of the New Testament these are called Justification and Sanctification. It is important to understand the meaning of these terms. "Justification," says the Catechism, "is an act of God's free grace, whereby He pardoneth all our sins and accepteth us as righteous in His sight, only for the righteousness of Christ, imputed to us and received by faith alone."

God's act in Justification by faith brings spiritual peace and a fresh start to the troubled human spirit, as in the notable case of Martin Luther. It is followed by the work of God, the Holy Spirit, who reshapes in God's likeness the life of the forgiven person giving him a fresh vision of life, and strength to fulfill it. This is the process of Sanctification, which is defined in these terms: "Sanctification is the work of God's free grace, whereby we are renewed in the whole man after the image of God and are enabled more and more to die unto sin and live unto righteousness."

Deeply moving is the description given in the Heidelberg Catechism of the state of mind of the man who has passed through a profound experience of Christian conversion and for whom Christ has become "all in all." Whereas the Westminster Catechism begins by raising the question as to the true end of human existence, asking, "What is the chief end of man?" the Heidelberg Catechism starts with a portrayal of the inward musings of the man who has begun to "glorify God and to enjoy Him forever." Listen to this spiritual rhapsody, one of the most remarkable combinations of poetry and theology in the whole range of religious literature. To the question "What is your one comfort in life and in death?", the answer is, "That I with body and soul, both in life and in death, am not my own, but belong to my faithful saviour Jesus Christ, who with his precious blood has fully satisfied for all my sins, and redeemed me from all the power of the devil; and so preserves me that without the will of my Father in Heaven, not a hair can fall from my head: indeed all things must minister to my salvation. Therefore by His Holy Spirit He also assures me of everlasting life and makes me willing and ready in heart henceforth to live unto Him."

This theological rhapsody has a twofold significance. Here the Lutheran and Reformed traditions meet. Here, too, is a classical expression of one of the two polar emphases of the Reformed tradition. One of these emphases is represented by the answer given to the first question of the Westminster Catechism. It says, in effect, man is truly man and fulfills his humanity when he makes it his life's objective to devote himself to God and to do His Will. The other emphasis is suggested by the closing words of the same answer "and enjoy Him forever." Here is struck the note of subjectivity, the note of Christian experience, of communion with God. This note is as classically Presbyterian as it is authentically Christian. For Presbyterians, too, throughout their history, have been as interested

in the inner life of the Christian as they have been in the outward expression of that life in theological thought and in God's
service in the Church and society. There have been times and
places in Presbyterian history when the crucial question asked
of a candidate for full Church membership, with its attendant
privilege of sitting down at the Lord's Table, was this: "What
reason have you for believing that you have been a subject of
divine grace and that you are truly a child of God?" It was
not necessary to be able to tell the day or the hour or even the
year of one's spiritual birth. The important thing was to be
able to give descriptive evidence of the working of God in the
soul in daily experience. To be able to do this qualified one
much more fully to be a "communicant" than did evidence of
doctrinal knowledge or ethical decency. The Church Session
was particularly concerned to discover whether the candidate seemed to belong to "the people of God, to the saints of
the most high."

Who are the "saints of the most high," and how are they
known? The remainder of this chapter will be devoted to a discussion of those aspects of Christian sainthood which have
received particular emphasis or expression in Presbyterian
thought and life.

THE MEANING OF SAINTHOOD

"You are called to be saints," said Paul to the Christians at
Corinth. "If that is so we must take our calling seriously," I
heard that distinguished Presbyterian theologian, James
Denny say, when I listened to him preach in boyhood days.
We are indebted to a great Anglican, J. B. Phillips, for his para-
phrased rendering of the meaning of sainthood. Saints are
"God's men and women," or what is the same, "Christ's men
and women."

The importance attached to the doctrine of Election in Presbyterian thought led inevitably to an emphasis upon the quality of life which was considered becoming for the "elect."
People who had reason to believe that God had made them

His own for a purpose, giving them a deep sense of calling, naturally strove to live worthily of Him who had called them. They became in the deepest sense "committed" people, men and women committed to God and responsive to His will.

Commitment to God in Jesus Christ has been a basic Presbyterian emphasis. To be maturely human in any sense of the term involves commitment to something bigger than one's self. The uncommitted life, let it be said frankly, is unworthy of a human being. It is quite as serious to live an uncommitted life as it is to live an "unexamined life," the life which a great Greek proclaimed to be unworthy of true men and women. Apart from out-and-out commitment to God there can be no true Christian life. That affirmation belongs to the core of classical Presbyterianism

Christian commitment is much more than admiration for Jesus Christ. It goes far beyond having orthodox ideas about Him. It is possible to vociferate the great doctrines about Christ without having any personal relationship to Christ. Committed Christians are loyal to the Church. They attend its services; they support its causes; they live in accordance with its requirements. But they do not confuse formal church membership with commitment to Jesus Christ. They belong to Him as their gracious Redeemer and sovereign Lord to whom they owe everything and to whom they give everything. Life has become for them no mere pursuit of happiness, no anxious effort to achieve success, no eager quest for inward peace. They do not use their religion to give them a social status. They do not confuse their religion with contributing to good causes. They do not equate their faith with patriotism. Belonging to Christ, they want to be Christlike, in the vocation which they follow and in every sphere in which they move. They are eager to serve Christ's cause in the world as members of the community of Christ, which is the Church. They will seek light upon their path of duty by having recourse to Bible study and prayer, to the counsel of fellow Christians, and to the wisdom which is enshrined in the Church's heritage of faith.

This they will do in humble dependence upon the Holy

Spirit, with an inner glow of enthusiasm, and with an outward demeanor of steady, unashamed, disciplined dedication to Christ and His cause. "Called to be saints," they will think and act as "Christ's men and women." They will do so in such a way as to bring the light and strength of the Eternal not only into the "daily round, the Common Task," but also into public spheres where life's problems and complexities are "new every morning." Even when official duties involve them in dealing with their country's enemies they will never be less than Christian in their bearing or attitudes, whatever be the occasion, or the issue, or the people involved.

Within the context of contemporary life, and especially in the sphere of public affairs, where Presbyterians have so often been called to play their part, "Christ's men and women" are challenged to manifest Christian freedom. They need to possess that insight and confidence which comes from Jesus Christ the Truth so that they shall not waver but act with decision.

But how true it is, alas, that in many instances today Presbyterians, too, become a prey to a current non-Christian mood, with its host of fears, prejudices and inhibitions. Some pride themselves so much in the wealth of ambiguities, ambivalences and dialectical tensions which they discover in human nature and contemporary life, that they maintain an Olympian detachment from the human struggle. They refuse to take sides lest they should take the wrong side. Enthusiasm and excitement they deem valid, as moods to be cultivated in secular life, especially in sport and politics; but in the sphere of religion they regard emotions of every kind with suspicion and disdain. And alas, alas, in some Presbyterian circles in the United States of America, and among representatives of the great Reformed tradition in South Africa, men and women are not accorded the dignity that God gave them in Creation and Redemption simply because their skins are black. Such an attitude on the part of Christians is a betrayal of Jesus Christ.

All such attitudes are aberrations from Christian sainthood. They are equally alien to the true genius of Presbyterianism, both in thought and in life. Let us listen to a great Presbyterian layman, George F. Kennan, one time American Ambassador to Moscow. Deeply aware of the fact that certain moral qualities are indispensable for true manhood, as well as for national greatness, and that the primary thing required of any nation is commitment to some absolute, Kennan said recently in Washington, "A country in the state this country is today, with no highly developed sense of national purpose, with the overwhelming accent of life on personal amusement, with a dearth of public services, and a surfeit of privately sold gadgetry, with an educational system where quality has been extensively sacrificed to quantity, if you ask me whether such a country has, over the long run, good chances of competing with a purposeful, serious, and disciplined society, such as that of the Soviet Union, I must say that the answer is 'No.' Implicit in this statement sounds the same tremendous question, "Freedom for what?"

"THE LIFE OF GOD IN THE SOUL OF MAN"

The inseparable correlative of commitment to God is communion with God. "Fellowship with the Father and with His Son, Jesus Christ" is a genuine experience of Christian "saints." To enjoy this fellowship is the constant aspiration of "God's men and women," and the abiding source of their spiritual vitality.

The reality of this holy communion is by no means limited to the eucharistic experience. It involves the still more mysterious reality of Jesus Christ becoming the very life of the Christian soul. It means to affirm with St. Paul, "I have been crucified with Christ, it is no longer I who live but Christ who lives in me." There is no adequate category with which to define this spiritual union in which Christ becomes the very life, even in an ontological sense, of his true disciple. It is in the depths of the soul where Christ has His dwelling that the severed Christian tradition becomes one and ecclesiastical boundaries and controversies are transcended. Said a character of Dostoevsky, the Russian novelist, "Someone came to my soul." In the experience of this coming, Theresa of Avila and John Bunyan are one.

Sometimes this intimate relationship with Christ is described as mysticism, a term which has not been popular recently in theological thought. Sometimes a manifestation of religious sentiment, or the affirmation that emotion belongs to the very essence of the Christian life, is disdainfully dubbed "piety" or "pietism" and even "piosity." Many people, even Presbyterians, have become desperately afraid of anything that verges upon the emotional and the lyrical in matters pertaining to Christian worship and witness. To be sedately religious is acceptable; to have it said of a person that he "has religion" raises serious questions regarding him.

The time has come to insist that deep religious emotion, which is something quite different from frothy, vociferous emotionalism, is native to Christian life and witness. To get excited about the salvation of one's soul, and when the occasion calls for it to talk, even to descant about what Jesus Christ has done for one and continues to mean to one, so far from this being alien to the Christian tradition, is integral to it. A reorientation is now due in Christian circles, and I am thinking particularly in Presbyterian circles, with regard to "The life of God in the soul of man." This phrase happens to be the title of a book written by a Presbyterian minister in the city of Aberdeen two centuries ago. Today, Arnold J. Toynbee, the historian, rightly reminds his contemporaries that "between saving one's soul and loving one's neighbor, there is no real antithesis."

Let me conclude this chapter by drawing attention to the fact that in the Presbyterian tradition great representative figures, giants in thought and action, were men of a very profound experience of the living reality of Jesus Christ as Saviour, and bore unashamed witness to it. I have a deep personal conviction that neither Presbyterians, nor Christians belonging to the traditional communions, can match the present hour in Church and society, unless we witness a rebirth of spiritual inwardness, a sense of Christ's Lordship in the soul, whatever be the name applied to this tremendous reality.

In an editorial which appeared in the October 1956 issue of *Theology Today*, entitled "Bonn 1930 and After, A Lyrical Tribute to Karl Barth," I wrote these words: "In our discussions in the old days in Bonn, I often became depressed and angry over Barth's disparaging references to Christian experience and to anything that had to do with so-called 'piety' or 'mysticism'—Karl Heim is alleged to have said of the Barth of that early period that what he needed most was a 'first-class conversion!' " The late Professor Koberle once said to me at a meeting in Utrecht, that when Barth came to deal seriously with the doctrines of the Person of Christ and of the Holy Spirit, his emphasis would change. I rejoice in the evidence that Karl Barth has moved beyond the abstract Kierkegaardian doctrine of the divine transcendance, which dominated so entirely his early thought, and has come to appreciate that form of subjectivity which emerges when a Christian can say with Paul, in profound self-abasement, "It is no longer I who live, but Christ Who lives in me."

I cannot but feel that among the Reformed churches of Continental Europe and also among the Presbyterian Churches in North America and around the world, there begins to be heard again the witness of the inner life. Testimony is being paid to the Lordship of Christ in the soul, which marked the lives of the most dynamic and creative figures in Presbyterian theology and churchmanship. Such are the issues and mood of our time that much more than theological clarity, ethical concern and liturgical loveliness are demanded. Contemporary theology and ethics must again sound the music of subjectivity.

Truly parabolic and prophetic in this connection are the words with which Karl Barth, the Neo-Calvinist, concludes his recent article in the *Christian Century* series "How my mind has changed." Says the Basel Professor: "I am not especially gifted or cultured artistically, and certainly not inclined to confuse or identify the history of salvation with any part of the history of art. But the golden sounds and melodies of Mozart's music have from early times spoken to me not as Gospel but as parables of the realm of God's free grace as revealed in the Gospel—and they do so again and again with great spontaneity and directness. Without such music I could not think of that which concerns me personally in both theology and politics, I could not even think of the decade of life whose happenings I have tried to relate here. There are probably very few theological study rooms in which pictures of Calvin and Mozart are to be seen hanging next to each other and at the same height."

✠ 5 ✠

The Presbyterian Understanding of the Church

Wнen the twentieth century was born, and for some time thereafter, very little was written about the Church. Christianity in general, Christ Himself, especially the historical Jesus, Christian experience and the Kingdom of God were the principal themes of theological discussion. In the twenties, soon after the close of the First World War, the Church began to become a theme of religious interest. Today, for a variety of reasons, the Church and everything connected with its doctrine, witness and relations, has come to occupy the center of the stage so far as Christian literature is concerned. The Church has been rediscovered.

Several things have contributed to this rediscovery. The birth of many new churches throughout the world as the fruit of the Christian missionary movement, the resolute witness of the Confessing Church of Germany, at a time when the German universities succumbed to the Nazi tyranny, the rebirth of Biblical theology with its recovery of the central category of the

Covenant and the "People of God," the birth of the Ecumenical Movement, the organization of the World Council of Churches, and the new quest to achieve the unity and fulfill the mission of the Church, all have contributed to the recovery in our time of a sense of the Church. A symbol of this recovery is the title of the most massive and important theological work since John Calvin wrote *The Institutes of the Christian Religion,* I mean, Karl Barth's *Church Dogmatics.*

A concept of the Church lies at the heart of Presbyterianism. To the consideration of that concept and its implications we now turn our thoughts.

THE COMMUNITY OF JESUS CHRIST

The Church, in simplest terms, is the community of those for whom Jesus Christ is Lord. Christ becomes Lord in the solitary depths of an individual human soul who responds to His call. This is the basic Lordship. But there is no place in Christianity for pure individualism. Nor is the Church made up of a diversity of persons, all of whom confess Christ, but each of whom affirms his independence of every other. The Church, it has been well said, is not found in the confessing individuals themselves, nor in each individual separately, but in all of them together. For the Christian Church is a community where Christians meet Christ and one another in Him. It is where two or three are met together in His name that Christ is present. But these two or three are members also of a vast community of which their little group is a part. This community is the creation of the Holy Spirit, who has founded upon "this Rock which is Christ," a society which can be variously called "The Holy Community," "The Congregation of the Elect," the "People of God," the "Holy Catholic or Universal Church."

The Church is primarily a fellowship and only secondarily an organization or institution. In this respect Presbyterians, and most other Protestant Christians, dissent from the Roman Catholic view of the Church. According to this view Christ founded His Organization; and in this Organization members of the clergy belong to the Church in a way that ordinary Christians do not. For Presbyterians, all Christians who confess Jesus Christ belong to the Church as the Community of Christ on terms of absolute equality. In the ultimate sense they are all priests.

The community must, of course, become organized, electing officers to whom are given special responsibilities. These officers are vested with special authority and looked up to with special reverence. But what constitutes the core or essence of the Christian Community as a whole is the awareness which the members possess of belonging together in the bonds of love and friendship. The sense of fellowship in Christ is much more basic to the reality of the Church than the participation in institutional privileges, the possession of ecclesiastical authority, or the development of a particular organizational structure.

This Community is the ultimate community, the Community of destiny. It constitutes God's central interest and agent in the unfolding of His eternal purpose for the world. The Church will outlive the rise and fall of empires and the coming and going of cultures and civilizations.

THE CHURCH: INVISIBLE AND VISIBLE

For Presbyterians, as for all who belong to the Reformed tradition, a clear distinction is to be drawn between the Invisible Church and the Visible Church. This distinction was very central in the thought of John Calvin, who found it embedded in the New Testament. In maintaining this distinction, Presbyterians differ from the teaching of the Roman Catholic Church, for which the Visible Church and the Invisible Church are one.

What is understood by the Invisible Church? The authoritative answer for Presbyterians is found in the Westminster Confession of Faith. Says the Confession: "The Catholic, or Universal Church which is Invisible, consists of the whole number of the elect that have been, are, or shall be, gathered into one, under Christ, the Head thereof, and is the Spouse, the Body, the fulness of Him who filleth all in all." The Church Invisible represents the whole company of the Redeemed, who have been, are and shall be the Bride and Body of Christ. In the contemplation of "all the Saints who from their labors rest," the Principalities and Powers in the heavenly places will, according to St. Paul, receive their deepest insight into "the many-colored wisdom of God." (Eph. 3:11)

It is the Visible Church, the Church militant on earth and in history, which especially concerns us at the present time. Presbyterianism has a high view of the empirical Church of which Christians, in their historical existence, are a part. Inspiring in spirit and significant in formulation is the Westminster statement regarding the Visible Church. It runs thus: "The Visible Church, which is also Catholic or Universal under the Gospel (not confined to one nation as before under the law), consists of all those throughout the world that profess the true religion, together with their children, and is the Kingdom of the Lord Jesus Christ, the house and family of God, through which men are ordinarily saved, and union with which is essential to their best growth and service."

Several things in this definition are worthy of note. The Visible Community of Christ in the world is equally Catholic or Universal. In our time this Community is actually "ecumenical," in the sense that its membership, albeit in nuclear form, is coextensive with the inhabited earth. It transcends all national, racial, cultural and ecclesiastical boundaries. The one requirement of a church body, in order to be considered a part of the "Holy Catholic Church" and as belonging to "the house and family of God," is that it should "profess the true religion." To "profess the true religion" means to belong to a church fellowship which gives it absolute allegiance to Jesus Christ as Lord and Saviour, and in which, as Calvin would put it, the Word of God is faithfully preached and the Sacraments rightly administered. There is, however, no perfect church. For, in the words of the Confession, "This Catholic Church hath been sometimes more, sometimes less Visible.

And particular churches, which are members thereof, are more or less pure, according as the doctrine of the Gospel is taught and embraced, ordinances administered and public worship performed more or less purely in them."

It is important to understand clearly what in this view constitutes the essence of churchly reality. For the Westminster divines, as for Calvin and for all who cherish the Reformed heritage of faith, a church is a Church of Christ, not because its ministers can validate a claim to be direct, main-line successors of the Apostles, nor yet because its members are paragons of holiness. Church members are called upon, of course, to approximate as closely as possible to being a "gathered church," by manifesting true piety, by professing sound doctrine and by living in accordance with the highest standards of morality. Its ministers are expected to be true shepherds of Christ's flock. It is, however, the true preaching of the Word, the due administration of the Sacraments, and the serious effort to worship God in public in the "beauty of holiness," and in a form consonant with His revealed will, that makes a Church to be a Church of Christ. This means that no church is absolutely pure. Says the Confession, with realism and sorrow, "The purest Churches under heaven are subject both to mixture and error," it then goes on to admit that "some (churches) have so degenerated as to become apparently no Churches of Christ."

Nevertheless, the unity of the Church should be maintained at all costs. From the Reformed viewpoint schism as such is an unmitigated evil which must never be glorified. A breach in Christian fellowship can be justified only in cases where Christians, by continuing in the membership of a given congregation or communion, would be forced into a position of absolute disloyalty to Jesus Christ and the Gospel. Under all ordinary circumstances, Christians should bear with fellow Christians who do not meet their standards, while striving by every means in their power to "teach them the way of the Lord more perfectly." They should realize, moreover, that the children of the great Mother have always been richly diversified in type. There have been, and always will be, in the Church Visible "Evangelicals" and "Moderates," "Pietists" and "Creedalists," "aesthetes" and "plain people." It is essential that all who are members of the one Body regard one another with "judgments of charity." It is but natural that Christians who are particularly congenial to one another, or who share special ideals to which they are devoted, should cultivate their common interests. But let them pursue their ideals and interests within the wider fellowship, let them not become sectarian in spirit or disrupt the unity of the Household of God. It is of the very genius of Presbyterianism that fellow Christians, who are concerned about the state of the Church or of their particular congregation, should remember that the Church with all its imperfections is the sphere of the grace of God, and that only in the Church is Christian sainthood possible. Let Christians stand, by all means, for discipline in the Church, but in so doing let them resist the disruption of the Church. Let it be their constant effort to achieve, by the grace of Christ, what was the consuming desire of John Knox in his time, "to bring back the grave and godly face of the primitive church." Their heritage bids Presbyterian Christians to be today what the Scottish Reformer wanted his fellow Presbyterians to be four hundred years ago, "the faithful congregation of Christ Jesus in Scotland."

CHRIST'S LORDSHIP IN THE CHURCH

A high Christology, an exalted view of Jesus Christ, not merely as a theological concept but as a living sovereign Presence in His Church, has marked the course of Presbyterian history.

"Jesus Christ is Lord." In these tremendous words St. Paul formulated the core of the Biblical message. Here is the first Christian creed in point of time and the most basic creed for all time. To affirm its timeless truth, and to live by its contemporary reality, is what alone entitles a person or a community of persons to claim the name of "Christian." The importance which Paul attached to this forthright affirmation is evident from his comment: "No one can say that Jesus is Lord but by the Holy Ghost." It is admittedly true that the word "lord" has an evil odor in the world of our time. In places where feudalism or colonialism still prevails, it has a hollow ring and many tragic overtones. In such a setting it is uttered as a term of conventional courtesy by persons who occupy an inferior status. When spoken under the shadow of totalitarian power the term has ominous and sinister associations. And yet, as a New Testament scholar has well said, "To enter into the meaning of this word, and give it practical effect, would be to recreate in great measure the atmosphere of the Apostolic age." Much more is needed, however, than to recreate the *atmosphere* of Apostolic Christianity in the interests of scholarly research. What is really needed, on the part of Presbyterian and all Churches, is to recreate the *reality* of Apostolic Christianity by incarnating in terms relevant to our time the truth of the timeless creed, "Jesus Christ is Lord."

To do precisely this has been a Presbyterian aspiration in the best days of our history since Calvin, Knox and Makemie. When, therefore, the ecumenical watchword is sounded today, "The Lordship of Christ in the Church and in the World," Presbyterians become concerned afresh to revive Apostolic Christianity in our time. This they seek to do by more intensive study of the Biblical records and of the annals of their own tradition.

Two recent happenings bear witness to the reawakened concern over Christ's Lordship in our time and nation which marks Presbyterian thought. At a crucial moment when it seemed as if the American state was about to formulate absolute standards of thought and behavior for the Christian churches and for all citizens in the nation there was issued by the General Council of the Presbyterian Church U.S.A. a document entitled "A Letter to Presbyterians Concerning the Present Situation in Our Country and in the World." In this document these words occur: "While being patriotically loyal to the country within whose bounds it lives and works, the Church does not derive its authority from the Nation but from Jesus Christ. Its supreme and ultimate allegiance is to Christ, its sole Head, and to His Kingdom, and not to any nation or race, to any class or culture. It is, therefore, under obligation to consider the life of man in the light of God's purpose in Christ for the world."

The second significant happening was the adoption by the World Presbyterian Alliance for the meeting of its Eighteenth General Council of the theme "The Servant Lord and His Servant People." Throughout the bounds of the Presbyterian world today, millions of people are seeking to understand afresh, and in terms of today, what it means to renew their allegiance to the great Head of the Church, the Sovereign Lord Jesus Christ Himself. Inasmuch as He Himself took the "form of a servant," He expects all the members of the Holy Community, which is His Body, to reflect the "servant image" in their life and work.

The Presbyterian concept of Church discipline derives directly from this high view of Christ's Lordship which has traditionally marked the Reformed churches. If it be true that "Jesus Christ is Lord," and that this Lord is personally present in the Sacrament of the Holy Supper, in order to communicate His life to those who partake of the symbols of His broken body and shed blood, no one should participate in this sacrament who is living in open or unconfessed sin, or leading a life that is unworthy of Christ. For that reason appropriate discipline must be exercised to exclude such a person from the privilege of sitting down at the Lord's table. For they alone are Christ's guests who alone render Him true allegiance. It was the effort to avoid the sacrilegious sham of people presenting themselves in Christ's presence at the Eucharistic feast, while denying Him by their lives, that led, in the earlier days of Presbyterianism, to the practice of "fencing the Table." Men were excommunicated from the fellowship of the Church, or were deprived of the privilege of being communicant members, not primarily because of some breach of ecclesiastical order, or even because they violated some ethical propriety as such, but rather as a consequence of their unrepentant denial of Christ's Lordship in personal behavior. Presbyterianism, when true to its native genius, attaches as much importance to the practice of Church discipline, whereby the scandalously unworthy are deprived of the privilege of participating in Christianity's most sacred rite, as it does to adding new members to the Church's fellowship.

CHRIST'S RIVALS AND PATRONS

In the course of the centuries, Presbyterians, like other Protestant Christians, have had to take issue with sundry powers that have disputed Christ's exclusive Lordship over His Church. The struggle against Papal domination in the sixteenth century, and subsequent efforts of the Church of Rome to reestablish its power in the British Isles, led the Westminster divines to include in the original Confession a very strong article against the headship of the Pope. This statement bears the scars of conflict and echoes the sentiment of the epoch. It runs, "There is no other head of the Church but the Lord Jesus Christ. Nor can the Pope of Rome in any sense be head thereof; but is that anti-Christ, that Man of sin, and son of perdition that exalteth himself in the Church against Christ, and all that is called God." American Presbyterians while being as resolutely opposed as their fathers to the papal pretension, and while becoming increasingly concerned regarding certain contemporary claims of the Holy Father, have phrased the traditional article in more delicate and Christian terms, as follows: "The Lord Jesus Christ is the only Head of the Church, and the claims of any man to be the vicar of Christ and the head of the Church are unscriptural, without warrant in fact and is a usurpation dishonoring to the Lord Jesus Christ."

In very recent times Presbyterians, out of their concern for Christ's Lordship in the Church, have become officially vocal regarding the trend in the Roman Communion to make the Virgin Mary a substitute for Jesus Christ in matters pertaining to the current events of history and the everyday concerns of the soul. So strongly did the Presbyterian General Assembly of 1955 feel on this matter that it issued a document entitled *The Lordship of Christ in Relation to the Marian Cult.* This manifesto contains these strong and significant words: "It is not that Mary becomes God, or that she is even an object of worship. It is rather that she represents God in dealing with men. In all that pertains to Christian salvation, to the achievement of human welfare and the establishment of peace on earth, she is the co-partner of Christ, His associate director, the virtual executive of the Holy Trinity."

In Scotland for nearly two centuries and in the United States until the early years of the eighteenth century, Presbyterians were obliged to challenge the authority of the state in the affairs of the Church. It should be remembered in this connection that the Church of Scotland, as well as the authors of the Westminster Confession, gave an authority to the state in relation to the Church which American Presbyterians have never accepted. All Presbyterians, everywhere and at all times, have been opposed to what in Church history is known as Erastianism. Erastianism is the doctrine that the State is a divine institution, whose responsibility it is to "provide for the dissemination of pure doctrine and for the proper administration of the sacraments and of discipline, and at the same time to support the Church, to appoint its officers, to define its laws and to superintend their administration." This view of state authority, which has been traditionally accepted by great Protestant churches on the continent of Europe, was at all times resolutely opposed by Presbyterians in the name of the sole Lordship of Jesus Christ over His Church, and in the interests of complete religious liberty.

At the same time the original Confession of Faith contained sentiments which American Presbyterians rejected in 1788. The early version stated: "The civil magistrate may not assume to himself the administration of the Word and Sacraments or the power of the keys of the kingdom of heaven: yet he hath authority, and it is his duty, to take order that unity and peace be preserved in the Church that the truth of God be kept pure and entire, that all blasphemies and heresies be suppressed, all corruptions and abuses in worship and discipline prevented or reformed, and all the ordinances of God duly settled, administered and observed."

When the First General Assembly of the Presbyterian Church in America convened in 1789 under the Moderatorship of John Witherspoon, this article was suppressed and the following substituted for it. The change breathes the spirit of American Presbyterianism, as well as the passion of Presbyterians for religious freedom for themselves and for all Christians. The new article which has continued in force reads thus: "Civil magistrates may not assume to themselves the administration of the Word and Sacraments, or the power of the keys of the Kingdom of Heaven: or in the least interfere in the matters of faith. Yet as nursing fathers, it is the duty of Civil Magistrates to protect the Church of our common Lord, without giving the preference to any denominations of Christians above the rest, in such manner that all ecclesiastical persons whatever shall enjoy the full, free, and unquestioned liberty of discharging every part of their sacred functions, without violence or danger. And, as Jesus Christ hath appointed a regular government and discipline in His Church, no law of any commonwealth should interfere with, let, or hinder, the due exercise thereof among the voluntary members of any denominations of Christians, according to their own profession and belief. It is the duty of civil magistrates to protect the person and good name of all their people, in such an effectual manner as that no person be suffered, either upon pretense of religion or of infidelity, to offer any indignity, violence, abuse or injury to any other person whatsoever; and to take order that all religious and ecclesiastical assemblies be held without molestation or disturbance."

Today, following the Union of 1929 between the Church of Scotland and the United Free Church of Scotland, the great mother Church of American Presbyterians has also won its spiritual freedom. While this Church is given special recognition by the British Government, the government possesses no authority whatever over the Church in the conduct of its work.

In this regard Scottish Presbyterianism has won for itself a freedom under the Lordship of Christ that is not yet enjoyed by some great sister churches of the Protestant Reformation.

Much more subtle, however, has been the insidious peril of powerful non-governmental patronage to which Presbyterian churches have been subjected and continue to be subjected. One of the most thrilling moments in the history of Scottish Presbyterianism was in 1843 when some five hundred ministers seceded from the Church of Scotland and literally walked out into the wilderness, rather than surrender their allegiance to Christ as the sole Head of the Church. Under the leadership of Thomas Chalmers, the greatest Scotsman since John Knox, the ministers refused to admit the right of landed proprietors, successors of the old feudal barons, to appoint ministers over Scottish parishes. Chalmers and his companions refused to surrender the right of Presbyterian congregations to elect their own pastors, under the Lordship of Christ alone. They surrendered instead everything that the world holds dear and suffered unspeakable hardship. It was then that the great Free Church of Scotland came into being.

American Presbyterianism has never had to contend with the religious authority of feudal lords; it has, however, had to contend, and never more than today, with the potent and much more subtle patronage of wealth. Historically, the capitalistic order was a creative development of Calvinistic principles in the world of business. Today, quite ironically, Presbyterian congregations, agencies and institutions find themselves under pressure from men of wealth to adopt policies or make promises which cannot be justified in terms of intelligent allegiance to Jesus Christ as Lord. Their benevolent patrons, themselves persons of Christian integrity, would insist that their particular viewpoint on social and political questions be adopted as a condition of their large gifts being bestowed.

This, of course, is not an exclusively Presbyterian problem. It is equally a problem of all Protestant denominations and even of the Ecumenical Movement. It is, however, an exceedingly delicate problem now that the Church has become so highly organized and so very expensive to operate. Tension frequently develops between the best judgment of responsible Christian leaders and the policy prescribed to them by men of wealth as a precondition of their resources being made available. In certain instances, the kindly, well-intentioned tycoon virtually assumes the role of Christ. Sometimes he, or a foundation which he has established, will launch or support religious enterprises which are by no means in the best interests of Christianity or the Church's witness. The time might well come when in a new form, and in the context of mid-twentieth-century America, the basic issue would have to be faced afresh which challenged Thomas Chalmers and his colleagues more than a century ago in Scotland.

Presbyterian church leaders recognize this peril. I have known cases in which the "Presbyterian Way" led to the deliberate and solemn rejection of gifts that would place in jeopardy the freedom of the Church and deprive its responsible leaders of their freedom to make decisions under the sovereign Lordship of Jesus Christ.

Still more insidious, however, is the threat to the Lordship of Christ in His Church by the new Communist attitude toward religion. Communism has come to recognize that it can further its cause much more effectively if it becomes, wherever possible, the patron of a Christian community rather than its persecutor. For by forthright persecution it creates for itself additional major problems. A notable instance of such patronage has appeared in Czechoslovakia. The historic and dedicated "Church of the Czech Brethren" is a member of the World Presbyterian Alliance. The present Czech government, which is a very intelligent and liberal Communist regime, has become the patron of Protestant Christianity in the country. It has gone out of its way to enshrine afresh in the sentiment and imagination of all Czech citizens the great figure of John Hus, the traditional national hero of the Czech people. A few years ago the government sponsored a film to interpret the life and death of Hus. It was a marvelous production in which the pre-Reformation churchman appears in the role of a great proletarian leader of the medieval period. In the course of time, the Reformer is arrested by the autocratic, anti-social Church authorities and condemned to death. While bound to the stake, and before the faggots are set ablaze, he is asked to recant. He refuses. Just as the flames envelop him he utters these words: "I cannot forsake my people."

It was my privilege to preach a sermon in the Hus Chapel, the first sermon to be preached there in more than three hundred years. The Communists had restored the ancient shrine where Hus was accustomed to preach and converted it into a museum. As a friendly gesture toward the Executive Committee of the World Presbyterian Alliance, which was holding its annual meeting in Prague, permission had been given to hold a religious service in this ancient sanctuary. From the old Hus pulpit and in the presence of some three thousand people, I preached the Gospel as clearly as ever I preached it in my life. Toward the close of the sermon, I congratulated the authorities on the marvelous film my companions and I had seen the night before. "I am not an authority on Czech history," I remarked, "but I do know that some eminent authorities affirm that the last words of John Hus at the stake were these: 'I cannot forsake my Christ.' But whether they were 'I cannot forsake my people' or 'I cannot forsake my Christ,' this we do know, John Hus, the great hero of Czech history, was a devoted disciple of Jesus Christ; and the man of Nazareth was the greatest lover of the common people who ever lived."

The new Communist patronage of religion may be insidious and have its perils. Any country, however, where a supreme lover of Christ and the people is allowed to be the chief national hero is predestined to awake some day to a great new period of human freedom. Through the Lordship of Jesus and the witness of the Church, which is His Body, the "shadows will flee away."

THE CHURCH, THE INSTRUMENT OF GOD'S GLORY

Presbyterianism from the beginning of its history has held a high view of the Church. What distinguishes the Church, however, as history's most unique community, does not lie in anything that inheres in its own nature or historical existence. The Church is the Community of Christ, and under Christ it will prove to be the community of destiny. It does not exist, however, for its own sake or for its own glory. It exists for God's sake. Its members, while enjoying fellowship with God and with one another, exist to give visible expression to God's character in their corporate and institutional life. They constitute the human medium within history through which God carries forward His great missionary purpose for mankind. To use a Biblical figure, it is the Church's glory, while exulting in all that God has done for the community of His Elect and enjoying His most intimate fellowship as sons and daughters of the Almighty, to accept the role of being God's servant.

"Let the Church be the Church" was the categorical imperative that resounded in 1937 at the Oxford Conference on "Church, Community and State," and which was soon to reverberate around the world. But when is the Church truly the Church? Despite claims and pretensions to the contrary, the Church is not truly the Church when either grandeur or status, prestige or power, are its chief concern. The Christian Church is the Church of Christ, only when, in the spirit and guise of its Lord and Master, it is willing to "take the form of a servant." It was as God's servant, according to the Old Testament, that Israel was to fulfill her destiny by being "a light to the nations," in order that salvation might "reach to the end of the earth." He who "thought not equality with God a thing to be grasped," proclaimed that he "came not to be served but to serve and to give his life a ransom for many." It was He who rose from a table after supper was over and assumed a traditional menial role. By washing their feet, He taught His disciples that their participation in His Body and Blood would become manifest in their willingness to "take the form of a servant." So it was too with Christ's greatest disciple. In writing to the Roman Christians St. Paul makes clear that he regarded his "servant" relationship to Christ as underlying and preceding the exercise of his Apostolic office. "Paul, a servant of Jesus Christ," he says, "called to be an Apostle, set apart for the Gospel of God."

It was to his "servants" that Christ gave the parting mandate "Go and make disciples of all nations," after he had made it clear that "all authority in heaven and on earth" had been given to him. As the representatives of the "New Israel" they were to carry God's salvation to the end of the earth. But He Himself never used his divine power for selfish purposes, but only for redemptive action and in the interests of others. So, too, all whom He admitted into intimacy with Himself, and for whom that power was available, were charged to validate the reality of their discipleship, not by claims and pretensions, but by their loyal obedience in action.

The Presbyterian influence out of which came the Oxford watchword, "Let the Church be the Church," was no more than the formal expression of what has always been an integral part of the Reformed heritage of faith. From Calvin's time onwards, it was regarded as the supreme glory of the Christian Church to be the agent of God's purpose in Christ. The Elect were chosen for service, not for privilege. The Visible Church, the historical Community of Christ, was designed to be the "Instrument of God's Glory." For that reason Presbyterians have consistently thought of the Church as being in the highest, holiest sense, instrumental in character. They believe that *mission* is of the very essence of the Church. They hold that nothing that the Church believes, or has, or claims to have, can make it truly the Church, unless it fulfills the mission with which it has been charged, and for the sake of which Christ dwells in the Church and imparts to the Church His power. In the highest sense both sermon and sacrament are designed to equip the Church for mission.

When therefore the World Presbyterian Alliance selected as the theme of "The Eighteenth General Assembly" "The Servant Lord and His Servant People," it did no more than recover for our time the image of the "servant" in relation to the role of the Church. In doing so it gave contemporary expression to the essentially instrumental, missionary character of the Church which is native to the Reformed tradition.

Of the Biblical figures which symbolize the intimate relationship between Christ and the Church, the Building, the Bride, the Body and the Flock, the one which is most deeply expressive of the Presbyterian emphasis upon the instrumental, dynamic way in which the Church is related to Christ is the figure of the Body. This figure, more than all the others, conveys the thought of Christ's redemptive, on-going action through the Church. It is the function of a human body to respond to the mandates of the head or to the impulses of the heart. So, too, with the Church as the Body of Christ. The Christian Church is truest to its nature when Christ, who is both its Head and its heart, uses His Body to save mankind through the Gospel, which the Church radiates as light and mediates as love.

All efforts to make the human body an end in itself violate the true nature of the body. Physical health, like mental acumen, is important, but not for mere public display. It is legitimate to cultivate by appropriate means the natural loveliness of the human organism. But to achieve national or international fame for bodily charm should not be the supreme objective of physical beauty. Muscular strength is worthy of development and can become impressive and spectacular. But physical prowess for its own sake is not a goal to be worthily pursued. In the life of a human personality the moment can come when health, beauty and strength may have to be joyously sacrificed for a cause. Responsive to the mandate of the head or an impulse of the heart, in loyalty to a great idea or a great cause, a body, a human personality, may have to die like a seedling in a furrow, if tomorrow is to witness a harvest of truth and righteousness. At the very core of the Christian religion, both as symbol and event, is the death of the body for the sake of something more important than the body.

So, has it often been with the Church as the Body of Christ. All too frequently the Church has made smooth functioning, organizational efficiency, harmonious relations among its numbers, or subscription to clearly defined creedal formulas, gleaming with orthodoxy, the supreme goal of its existence. Sometimes it has gloried in the architectural beauty and grandeur of the sanctuaries where the worship of God has been carried on, or in the impressiveness of a liturgical service to which every aesthetic device has been made tributary. Many a time the Church has made the acquisition of power its supreme objective, striving to gain influence and prestige by purely secular methods and for purely secular ends. In all these cases the Christian Church has sacrificed its spiritual character by becoming a Kingdom of this world.

The Church as the Body of Christ can be true to its nature only when it carries out Christ's mission in the world and for the world. In no sense dare it live for its own glory, but for His. Never must the Church allow itself to gloat upon the fact that it is the Body of Christ in such wise as to engender pride and lead to boastful claims. Rather must it be true to its calling and fulfill its mission. This it must do in a spirit of absolute obedience to Christ, adjusting itself to the realities of the situation in which it finds itself, winning thereby a right to be heard and to be taken seriously. The Church of Christ must never become conformed to any culture or civilization; rather must it, in a pilgrim spirit, be ever moving forward and beyond.

It can truly be said that the pilgrim, crusading character of the Christian Church, which God designed as the true mark of the Old Israel and the New, and which belongs to the historic witness of Presbyterianism, has begun again to stir the Presbyterian soul. The first action taken by the General Assembly of 1958, which was the First Assembly of the newborn

Church, the United Presbyterian Church in the United States of America, was to approve a document entitled "In Unity for Mission." This document was ordered to be read in every congregation of the United Church. It contains a vivid, contemporary summary of Presbyterian doctrine as regards the instrumental missionary nature of the Church.

This is what it says: "The Church is truly the Church when it serves God, when God's sons and daughters become their Father's servants. It is all too easy for the Church to become a venerated but sterile institution in the society in which it exists. Neither the Church itself, nor any of its achievements, whether its structure or its doctrine, its unity or its work, can ever be mere ends in themselves; all are but means to serve the ongoing purpose and redemptive love of God.

"The Church must be a pilgrim Church. God summons us to pilgrimage, to life on the missionary road. We must journey not only along desert paths and jungle trails, but in the teeming alleys of our cities. God commands us to be missionaries not only in the community where we live, not alone in the national environment of our home church, but to the ends of the earth. The Church's place is the frontier. But for the Church in the discharge of its God-given mission, the frontier is more than a location. It is wherever any sector of thought or life has to be occupied in the name of Jesus Christ.

"Only as church members become Christ's missionaries in their several vocations, in government and diplomacy, in industry and commerce, in the home and in the classroom, in the clinic and on the farm, will men perceive that Christ is *the* Way, *the* Truth, and *the* Life.

"We are haunted by our Lord's own question, 'What do ye more than others?' Our Lord calls the Church to unqualified obedience. The measure of our obedience is the measure of our power. Let the Church demonstrate by the consistency of its life the validity of its claims.

"This we call upon our churches to do. Every congregation should be a reflection of the Holy, Catholic Church. In Christ, racial, cultural, social, economic, and sex distinctions become meaningless and are erased. Each congregation is called upon to evangelize and to welcome into its membership all the un-churched people of its community without regard to their racial, economic, or cultural background and condition.

"Let us, therefore, implore our Father in Heaven for a fresh outpouring of His Spirit upon us. We pray that this union will mark the beginning of that spiritual awakening which our Church, and all the Churches, and the whole human family, so sorely need in this hour.

"Jesus promised his followers that he would be with them in holy companionship to the end of the road, to the close of the age. As we gird ourselves for our pilgrimage, our courage is His pledge. And, as we journey, our strength is in the imperishable hope that the kingdoms of this world shall become the Kingdom of our Lord and of His Christ.

"The grace of our Lord Jesus Christ be with us all."

PART TWO

The Presbyterian Pattern
Of Life

✠ 6 ✠

Church Order

Every church has a structure of some kind. It is organized according to a definite pattern, with an orderly system of relations and a specific method of functioning. Without adopting a discernible shape, simple or complex, acceptable to its members, the Community of Christ could not possibly carry on in the sense which has already been discussed.

In the course of Christian history, there have been three main views regarding the status of order or structure in the life of the Church. It has been maintained that structure, a concrete form of ecclesiastical order, *is* the Church. This is the Roman Catholic view. According to this view, Jesus Christ founded "His Organization." This Organization is constituted by a hierarchy of clergy, whose members *are* the Church, belonging to it in a manner in which the rank and file of the faithful do not.

According to a second view, structure is of the *essence* of the Church. It is held that, apart from a form of organization in which the clergy, especially bishops, have a status and authority not shared by the laity, a church cannot truly be regarded as a church. This is the view held by the Eastern Orthodox churches and by communions commonly called "High Church."

The third view affirms that *structure is structure*. According

115

to this view, structure neither constitutes the Church, nor is it the essence of the Church. It exists as the servant of the Community of Christ to enable the Community to function in the most effective way possible, while fulfilling its God-given mission under the Lordship of Jesus Christ.

Presbyterians, and all Christians in the World Alliance of Reformed Churches, accept the third view of the essentially functional character of Church order. For Presbyterians, the Church is composed of all those for whom Jesus Christ is Love. Its members have the status of "priests," in harmony with the Reformation doctrine of the "priesthood of all believers," and so are all equal before God. They enjoy the same privileges and partake of the same responsibilities. Clergy and laity together constitute, upon an equal basis, "the people of God," whose life must be lived under God and for God. The structure, therefore, which gives organizational form to their life must, in the truest and most dynamic sense, serve to develop and express this life. In a word, Church structure is for the life of the Church community. It is not an end in itself. It does not exist in its own right. This is the genius of Presbyterian order.

STRUCTURE IS FOR LIFE

Let it not be thought however that Presbyterians apply to the structure and government of the Church a purely pragmatic criterion, judging organization exclusively by the results it achieves. From the days of Calvin and Knox, it has been the concern of Presbyterians to validate their conception of Church order by a direct appeal to Holy Scripture. Unlike Luther, Calvin believed that the New Testament presents an essential pattern for the organization of Christ's Church. This pattern Christians should regard as normative. Luther, on the other hand, while believing that the Bible is the sole authoritative source for Christian doctrine, held that it was not intended to provide Christians with a normative pattern, either for Church order or for the conduct of public worship. Calvin, and Presbyterians after him, have held that there are basic principles in the New Testament by which Christians should be guided in the organization and worship of the Christian Community.

While Calvin claimed that the Church order which he introduced into the Protestant community of Geneva approximated most closely to the authoritative New Testament pattern, he hastened to add that other Christians might find a different pattern in the Apostolic records. Provided Christians took the New Testament seriously as their ultimate guide in organizing and governing the Church, Calvin would allow them the utmost freedom in giving concrete expression to the fruit of their study. This meant that for him, as for Presbyterians in the great Calvinistic tradition, no given form of Church order is of the essence of the Church. The New Testament foundation and the binding validity of a given Church order must, therefore, be determined by the manner and degree in which it serves to edify, that is to build up the Church, the People of God.

Two things are to be noted. Truth must always, of course, have the priority. Christians must maintain an abiding concern that the Church's structure and functioning shall be inspired by Biblical principles and patterns under the guidance of the Holy Spirit. For it is the Spirit who leads the Christian into ever new discoveries of the Eternal Truth. On the other hand, nothing that the Church is or does shall be for its own sake, for the simple promotion of its own institutional interests, nor yet for the sake of any alien power that attempts to make the Church the instrument of its will. Everything must be for the glory of God in the "upbuilding of the saints," that they in their turn may fulfill their ministry. That is to say, the Church's "servant" or instrumental function is the key to the interpretation of Presbyterian Church order.

Thus the Church, in loyal obedience to Christ, its Head, and being structurally patterned upon Biblical models, while at the same time never presuming to proclaim its own or any other organizational form as the only God-given shape for Christ's Church, shall strive to perform its essential God-given functions. This the Church shall do in such a way, that in its organized life the functions it must fulfill shall always be regarded as more important than the offices it must fill.

The two poles in the organized structure of Presbyterianism are the Local Congregation, with its Church Session, and the General Assembly. The Local Congregation is made up of a community of Christians who have elected officers consisting of elders, deacons, trustees and a minister or ministers. These officers attend to the spiritual and temporal needs of the people and give them leadership in the fulfillment of their corporate functions. The General Assembly, which is made up equally of clergy and laity, ministers and elders, on a representative basis, is vested with authority to deal with matters that concern the life and work of the Church as a whole. We will examine, in a moment, the whole Presbyterian structure of which the Local Congregation and the General Assembly are pivotal powers. In order, however, that this may be done intelligently and in due historical perspective, let me refer briefly to the difference between the birth of Presbyterianism in Scotland and in the United States.

In Scotland, in the sixteenth century, Presbyterianism came into being as a General Assembly. In the United States, on the other hand, it first appeared in the seventeenth century in the form of Local Congregations.

It was a dramatic moment in Scottish history when the National Parliament authorized John Knox and those who, under his leadership, had broken away from the Roman Catholic Church to come together in a Church Assembly. The Assembly was given authority to organize its life in its own way. The great movement thus begun in the English speaking world stood for three revolutionary principles. *First,* the Church lives and must carry on its work under the supremacy of God. *Second,* the rights of the laity and the solidarity of the human kind must be maintained. *Third,* the divine right of men must take the place of the divine right of kings. The new Church order that thus came into being created the spirit which in later times inspired Kipling's famous lines:

"The people, Lord, the people,"
"Not thrones, nor crowns but men."

This spirit of Calvin and Knox was to resound two centuries later in the American Colonies. In the meantime, the Scottish General Assembly of 1560 took steps to organize congregations throughout the country. Because of the historical situation in which Presbyterianism in Scotland was born, it is natural that the General Assembly in the land of Knox should possess more traditional power than in the adopted country of John Witherspoon.

The origin of Presbyterianism in the United States was quite different. It moved from the bottom up and not from the top down. It is but natural, therefore, that in the American Presbyterian tradition Local Congregations, which found themselves from the beginning in a missionary situation, should continue to reflect in their organization and spirit the circumstances of their birth. Two significant facts may be mentioned.

From the beginning the question of financial support for congregational work was a greater problem in America than in Scotland. In Scotland the Church inherited certain titles to lands and properties and, being the established Church, it could count upon the support of the state. But the situation in the New World was quite different. There emerged in American Presbyterianism the Trustee and the Board of Trustees. Trustees are laymen who may or may not be elders. They control the Church's financial policies. Where necessary, they constitute a holding corporation, so that the congregation may be able to own property in accordance with state law. The Trustees symbolize the fact that all money matters are in the hands of the laity and not of the clergy. The minister of a congregation, while he may sit in with the Board of Trustees, is not necessarily a member of the Board in terms of constitutional right. In Scottish Presbyterianism financial matters on the congregational level are in the hands of the Deacon's Court, a judicatory which is presided over by the minister and is made up of members of the Church Session together with the duly elected deacons.

A second significant fact is this. In American Presbyterianism ordained ministers cannot be members of Local Congregations. In consequence, they can hold no congregational office. A minister's wife can be a member of a local church. Her husband, however, who may be a seminary professor, the secretary of one of the denomination's Boards or agencies, or be simply a retired clergyman living in the locality, cannot be a member, far less an officer, of the congregation where he worships and which he supports. The minister's relationship is to the Presbytery. In Scottish Presbyterianism it is different. Theological professors, and ministers not active in a pastoral sense, can be both members and officers of a local church. In American Presbyterianism there exists a constitutional wariness of clerical domination or control, just as there has been a corresponding wariness about vesting too much power in the General Assembly. In some instances, because of special historical circumstances or local conditions, symptoms of positive congregationalism and laicism have developed.

What I have said in this section points up to this. There is order and flexibility, but no canonized absolutism in the organized structure of Presbyterianism. It has been true from the beginning and continues to be true today, that the structure of the Church is for the life of the Church.

THE SOVEREIGN PEOPLE AND THEIR ELECTED OFFICERS

All who have been baptized as infants are regarded as belonging to the Visible Church. Those only, however, who have made a profession of personal faith in Christ and are in full communion with the Church as communicant members, have the privilege of partaking of the Sacrament of the Lord's Supper, together with the privilege of voting at congregational meetings. If an applicant for communicant membership should not have been baptized as a child, baptism by profession of faith must precede his admission to the Church as a member in full communion. This procedure is consistently followed even when the candidate for membership is the President of the United States. At the same time, a person becomes a full communicant and voting member in the Presbyterian Church without the necessity of subscribing to any elaborate statement of belief such as is required of officers of the Church. The crucial question which all candidates for membership must answer affirmatively is this: "Do you confess your faith in God, the Father Almighty, Maker of heaven and earth, and in Jesus Christ, His only Son, our Lord, and do you promise, with the aid of the Holy Spirit, to be Christ's faithful disciple to your life's end?" Those who make this confession and promise to live out its implications as loyal members of the local church fellowship have the privilege and responsibility of electing the diverse officers who by their election are vested with authority in the "Community of Christ."

As to the personal life and witness of those who make this profession of faith, there is as much variety among Presbyterians as there is among the members of other Christian communions. There are congregations whose members reflect in their individual life, and in their corporate witness, the characteristics of the "gathered Church at its best." And let this not be forgotten. The concept of the "gathered Church," the Church made up of members who are totally committed Christians and who give evidence by the quality of their witness that they are "Christ's men and women," is native to historic Calvinism. It constitutes an ideal toward which all Presbyterian Churches should strive, provided they do so in the unsectarian, ecumenical spirit which is enshrined in the Reformed tradition.

It has to be admitted, on the other hand, that there are Presbyterians who, in their church relations and secular calling, are more obsequious to the "American way of life" than they are to the Christian or the "Presbyterian way." Some of these are Christ's patrons and not his servants. They use His name because it enjoys prestige, but they fail to do His Works; for to take Christ seriously would involve them in unpopularity. Others, while being nominally church members, are in reality church alumni. They assume little or no responsibility in the organized work of the congregation. Only very occasionally are they present at public worship. They glory, nevertheless, in their church affiliation and support the Church in an impersonal and material way. They know the historic names of Calvin, Knox and Witherspoon. Like good alumni, they appear in the sanctuary on the great festive occasions of the Christian year. Many members of Presbyterian churches are in fact God's grandchildren, if the term may be allowed, and not His immediate sons and daughters. They are second, third, or nth generation Presbyterians. They enjoy belonging to a religious tradition and are proud of their religious heritage, but they know nothing of an intimate family circle where the children, when gathered together, say with great naturalness, "Father," to the one to whom they owe their being. All of which means that in Presbyterian congregations, as in congregations belonging to other communions in the contemporary church, there is urgent need of renewal. An evangelistic task waits to be done. "Judgment must begin at the House of God."

In view of the complex situation that prevails in congregational life today in the historic Christian churches, it becomes clear that an unusual responsibility devolves upon the Church's ministers.

THE MINISTER

First and foremost among the officers whom the people elect to "be over them in the Lord," is the minister or pastor. It is presupposed that the person who is called by a congregation to be its minister has met all the necessary requirements. In addition to the personal qualities which have commended him to his prospective "flock," he is presumed to be a man who has felt himself called by God Himself to the work of the holy ministry. He must also have met the standards prescribed by his denomination for ministerial candidates. This must be done to the satisfaction of the Presbytery under whose care his preparation has been carried on, and whose responsibility it is to license and ordain him as a minister of the Gospel.

In addition to the constitutional questions of a doctrinal character which a candidate for ordination must answer, and to which reference was made in Chapter 2, he is required to give affirmative answers to other questions that relate not to his theological position, but to the "way of life" which is expected of him as a Presbyterian minister. The future minister is confronted with the following:

> "Do you approve of the government and
> discipline of the United Presbyterian Church
> in the United States of America?
>
> Do you promise subjection to your brethren
> in the Lord?
>
> Have you been induced, as far as you know
> your own heart, to seek the office of the holy
> ministry from love of God and a sincere
> desire to promote His glory in the Gospel of
> His Son?
>
> Do you promise to be zealous and faithful in maintaining
> the truths of the Gospel and the purity and
> peace of the Church whatever persecution or
> opposition may arise unto you on that account?
>
> Do you engage to be faithful and diligent in the
> exercise of all your duties as a Christian and
> a minister of the Gospel, whether personal or
> relative, private or public and to endeavor
> by the grace of God to adorn the profession
> of the Gospel in your manner of life, and to
> walk with exemplary piety before the flock of
> which God shall make you overseer?"

Satisfactory answers having been made, the new minister kneels. The ministerial members of the Presbytery, under whose auspices he is being ordained and installed, lay their hands upon his head, according to the Apostolic example, while prayer is offered by the presiding minister. In this way "He is set apart to the holy office of the Gospel ministry."

Ordination in the Presbyterian concept does not mean that the man upon whom the "hands of the Presbytery" are laid becomes the recipient of special grace through that act. Nor yet does it mean that he becomes, thereby, a qualitatively superior type of being, different from all other Christians, as is maintained in the Roman conception of the Priesthood. It means, rather, that he has been set apart for the fulfillment of a special function. The fulfillment of this ministerial function involves a task and an office. Through the worthy discharge of his task and the conscientious occupancy of his office, with all the privileges and the responsibilities pertaining thereto, a Presbyterian minister derives his authority from the office he fills and from the stature of his own personality, and not from any claim to be a religious "superman," or yet to represent to a new category of being.

As regards ordination, Presbyterians are insistent upon two things: 1) The act of ordination, as already stated, does not create a new order of spiritual being. Before God the ordained minister does not occupy a higher rank in the scale of human reality than does an ordinary Christian. 2) Presbyterian ordination, whereby a man becomes "a minister of the Word and Sacraments," claims complete validity in the Church of Christ. For that reason, no Presbyterian Church will ever enter into organic union with any other church which disputes the validity of Presbyterian orders. Presbyterians will not accept the demand that as a precondition of union, Presbyterian ministers shall be re-ordained, or at least submit to the hands of a bishop being laid upon them. In this connection it should be observed, however, that there is nothing in Presbyterianism which would preclude the designation "bishop" ("overseer") being applied to a minister who was elected to a position of special authority and, to the office of "superintendent," for example. Whatever superiority can be predicated of one ordained minister over another does not inhere in the man himself but derives solely from the office. All ministers of Christ are peers, and anyone elected to a position of particular eminence is "a prince among equals" (*Princeps inter pares*).

For the same reason the usual hierarchical question regarding Apostolic Succession has neither meaning nor validity for Presbyterians. What matters in the Church of Jesus Christ is not whether the claim can be substantiated that certain members of the clergy are able to trace their ecclesiastical descent back to the Apostles. The real issue is this: Can Christian ministers give positive proof that they are dedicated to, and are actually carrying forward the missionary task of the Apostles? This Apostolic task is to be carried forward today in local parishes as well as on the great frontiers of the Kingdom. The ordinary minister in his parish, who worthily engages in the work of a pastor, teacher and evangelist, is a much truer successor of the Apostles than a proud, scarlet-gowned ecclesiastic who merely glories in his high office. Spiritual community with the Apostles in their mission, and not hierarchical continuity with them in their office, is what makes Christian ministers their successors.

With this we return to the new minister in his parish. What we found to be true of church members is true also of their ministers. What pastors prove to be in relation to God, to their people, and to the community at large, will depend upon these three factors: the quality of their spiritual life, the interpretation they give to their ministerial tasks, and the perspective in which they regard a minister's relationship to the secular community.

Presbyterianism has emphasized the Lordship of Christ over the Church and the world; it has also stood for the Church's responsibility toward the secular order. For that reason its clergy, as well as its laity, have tended to be socially minded.

MINISTERIAL TYPES

Very early in Presbyterian history in Scotland there appeared two main types of minister, each claiming to be a true representative of the "Presbyterian Way." One type put the emphasis upon the claims of the soul, the other upon the claims of society. The members of the one group were supremely concerned about personal religion, the "life of God in the soul of man," and the work of Evangelism. They were called "Evangelicals." The members of the other group were supremely concerned about society's appreciation of the Church and its due acceptance of the clergy. They stood for high ethical principles, but they were definitely opposed to anything that had the semblance of religious enthusiasm or emotion. They were less interested in the transformation of society by the Gospel than they were that society should recognize that ministers of the Gospel were good fellows; that they had cultural interests and a cultivated taste and were worthy of admission in the best social circles. These men were called "Moderates." In Scotland during the eighteenth century and the first half of the nineteenth, the Church of Scotland witnessed an ever-present tension between "Evangelicals" and "Moderates."

From the religious annals of the Scottish Highlands in the eighteenth century, I cull two descriptive gems which are parables of the two Presbyterian types just referred to. The wife of a "Moderate" minister reported to her husband that many members of his congregation were leaving the congregation and were going to attend services each Sabbath in the neighboring parish. His reply was "Look if you can see any of them with my stipend on his back." A famous "Evangelical" pastor in Lochcarrom, the parish of my own ancestors, who was a legendary figure for his piety as well as a man of culture and fine humor, is the author of this gay stanza:

> "The parson has no home nor farm
> No goat nor watch nor wife;
> Without an augmentation to
> He leads a happy life."

These may be symbols of dialectical extremes, but they represent real and abiding types. They embody lessons for all Presbyterians today who are concerned about the ministerial calling.

In Scottish Church history there is another parabolic figure who offers a pattern for all Christian ministers in our time and country. He is Thomas Chalmers, the leader of the famous Disruption of 1843, one of the most symbolic and creative movements in Presbyterian history. Chalmers, a young minister, who was also a brilliant mathematician, aspired to the Chair of Mathematics in Edinburgh University. It was his contention that a minister of the Church of Scotland could adequately fulfill all the duties of his office in two days of the week and so be able to devote the remaining five days to any avocation he might choose. Academic pundits, he maintained in an anonymous pamphlet, should not hold against him "the stigma of ordination." This was a characteristic Moderate thesis.

It happened, in the meantime, however, that this young, Moderate minister passed through a profound experience of conversion. After the "great change," Chalmers continued to live on the frontiers of cultural and social concern in a more intensive manner than ever. But his attainments in astronomy, political science, and the new science of economics were put to the service of Christ and His Church. Years later, a heated debate took place in the General Assembly of the Church of Scotland on the question of "pluralities." It was being contended on the floor of the Assembly that a minister could engage formally and for wages in secular activities, and at the same time give due attention to all his ministerial duties. Every eye was turned on the venerable figure who had once been the champion of the thesis that for any ordinary, intelligent person the parish ministry was a part-time job. Chalmers paused and rose. What he said is cherished as one of the most memorable utterances ever delivered in the Scottish General Assembly. It has ringing overtones for the Presbyterian ministry today. "I was at that time, sir, more devoted to mathematics than to the literature of my profession. And feeling aggrieved and indignant at what I conceived, an undue reflection upon the abilities and education of our clergy, I came forward with that pamphlet to rescue them from what I deemed an unmerited reproach, by maintaining that a devoted and exclusive attention to the study of mathematics was not dissonant to the proper habits of a clergyman.

"Alas, sir, so I thought in my ignorance and pride. I have now no reserve in saying that the sentiment was wrong, and that in the utterance of it, I penned what was outrageously wrong. Strangely blinded that I was! What, sir, is the object of mathematical science? Magnitude and the proportions of magnitude. But then, sir, I had forgotten two magnitudes. I thought not of the littleness of time, I recklessly thought not of the greatness of eternity."

I have gone back into the history of Scottish Presbyterianism because the Presbyterian "way of life" in old Caledonia has many lessons to teach Presbyterian ministers who would tread the Christian way in America and in the world of our time. The Christian way alone is the absolute way. As regards the "Presbyterian Way," it must be more than a mere description of what that way has been or is; it must also be a vision of what that way *should* be in a time like ours when no way is completely clear.

This much is plain, however, whether the work of the ministry is carried on in an urban or a rural area, in the inner city or in the growing suburbia, on a university campus, in hospital wards, or military camps: there is guidance for the Presbyterian Way today in the great tradition of yesterday and in the abiding contemplation and fellowship of that Pilgrim who is, Himself, the Everlasting Way, Jesus Christ our Lord.

Out of the Scottish past comes yet another inspiration. "Lord, grant true pastors to thy flock," said John Knox in one of his last prayers. To be a pastor, to have a shepherd's heart, to be sensitive to human need, to know out of one's own faith and experience how to meet this need, without having to recur everlastingly to a psychiatrist, is or should be the "way" of the Presbyterian minister. Were the Good Shepherd always followed in our time by his under shepherds, agitated human spirits would be given spiritual food as well as psychological diagnosis and advice. They would be introduced to the divine Redeemer and not chiefly to that new Divinity whose name is the Analytical.

An echo of the Scottish issue between "Moderates" and "Evangelicals" was heard in Pennsylvania and New Jersey more than two centuries ago. Gilbert Tennent, the son of the founder of the famous Log College, preached a sermon entitled "An Unconverted Ministry." It caused an ecclesiastical uproar. Tennent, it is true, was unduly scathing in his language and much too withering in his indictment of a certain type of clergyman. This he subsequently acknowledged with deep regret. On the other hand, he raised an inescapable issue to which Presbyterianism has always been alive. In terms of human personality and experience, and not merely in terms of theological formulation, what is meant by "redemption," "regeneration," "conversion," and "new birth"?

Amid the chaotic welter of values in our purposeless society, the clear evidence that representatives of upstart groups without history or tradition, are making a deeper impact upon contemporary man throughout the world than do the more staid and cultured representatives of the historic churches, raises questions which are delicate and not easy to answer. So far as Presbyterians are concerned, let this be said. It is not un-Presbyterian, but is truly Presbyterian, and in the classical Reformed tradition, that a minister should "maintain the spiritual glow" in every sphere where he moves, beginning with that ultimate arena of creative encounter, the Local Congregation. It is fitting, therefore, that a man upon whose head the "hands of the Presbytery" were laid, as he knelt in lowliness, should examine himself. And let the Presbyterian minister who writes these lines lead the way.

Studies that have recently been made of the minister and his problems, and of the image which Presbyterians and other ministers have of themselves and their work, have brought out some facts of crucial importance. Such is the setup in American Protestant Churches that the present-day minister tends to be swamped in administrative responsibilities. He has tended to take on the pattern that is most current in secular society, and has become an "organization man." The task of assuring smooth functioning and efficient order in the work and relations of the multiple groups into which his people are divided, makes it difficult for the average minister to be a preacher and a shepherd as well as an administrator. The only answer to this problem is that the minister mobilize all the lay talent in the congregation and distribute the total ministerial task among "God's men and women," over whom he has been made the "overseer."

The ultimate solution of this problem is the recovery of something that lies deep in the Presbyterian heritage. Let the laity, both men and women, have equal responsibility with the minister in caring for the "Community of Christ." They, too, must be shepherds and preachers, teachers and administrators, according to their several gifts and opportunities. The ultimate criterion of success in the pastoral ministry is to achieve the goal envisioned by St. Paul. In the course of his letter to the Christians at Ephesus, Christ's greatest minister said in effect this: The supreme objective for which specially commissioned and ordained officers have been given by Christ to His Church is this, "in order to equip His people for the work of serving," that is, that they, too, in the deepest and most Christian sense, should be ministers (Eph. 4:11, 12). The laity also must be servants of Him who came "not to be served but to serve." To recover this forgotten aspect of the "priesthood of all believers," is for Presbyterians and their fellow Christians to follow the "Way."

FROM KIRK SESSION TO GENERAL ASSEMBLY

The chief governing body in a Local Congregation is the Session. It is composed of the minister, who presides, together with a group of "ruling elders." The latter are elected by the congregation from among members in full communion and are inducted into office by ordination, with the laying on of hands and "the right hand of fellowship." The number of elders will depend on the size of the congregation, but in every instance a Session must be composed of at least a minister and two elders.

THE ELDERSHIP

The Session is responsible for the complete oversight of congregational affairs and has authority to exercise discipline. New communicant members must be approved by the Session. The elders assist the minister in the administration of the Lord's Supper by personally conveying the sacred elements to the members, who remain seated in the pews. When a Session functions in accordance with the true tradition of Presbyterian order, the elders share with the minister the responsibility of exercising pastoral care by visiting the sick. In the early days of Presbyterianism the eldership constituted a life office and continues to be so in many Presbyterian Churches. In American Presbyterianism, however, the rotary principle has been introduced in recent years so that the personnel of the Session changes continually and power remains no longer in the hands of any one group.

There is an element of uniqueness in the Presbyterian eldership. Historically its emergence restored to Christianity a long lost and forgotten office which was represented by those elders of the Church in Ephesus who visited Paul at the seaport of Miletus. They received from him the commission to "feed the Church of God in which," as he put it, "the Holy Spirit has made you guardians" (that is, "overseers" or "supervisors"). In secular society the advent of the "elders" spelt the elevation of the common man to a new dignity and sense of vocation. This point has been admirably made by a very distinguished Church historian, recently deceased, Professor S. G. Henderson of Aberdeen University. Says Dr. Henderson in his outstanding study of Presbyterianism, "In the eldership Renaissance individualism was consecrated to the service of Christ and to Christian witness in the world. The Reformed scheme not only endowed the layman with a new sense of vocation in his ordinary occupation and his home life, but brought to his notice rights and responsibilities in connection with organized religion. The new, devout, educated layman, as well as his simpler but equally pious peasant brother, was given a place of dignity and opportunity as not only a member but as an ordained office-bearer in the Church representing his fellow members. The Christian cause was strengthened at a critical period by winning for its active service the splendid spiritual resources of the laity."

Throughout Presbyterian history the "elders," who, in certain periods and places, have been called with awe and reverence "the men," have played a very decisive part in Church affairs. They have also preached, without any special commission, in the interests of the cause. In American Presbyterianism elders have frequently been "Moderators" of the General Assembly. In recent times the presence of women as well as men in the eldership of some Presbyterian Churches has greatly enhanced the stature and increased the influence of Church Sessions and the historic eldership.

In close association with the Session functions in each congregation is a "Board of Deacons." The "deacons" are charged especially with administering the temporal affairs of the congregation, the promotion of philanthropy and the care of those members who are in need of financial aid, or have special temporal problems. The "deacons," who carry forward the great tradition of "diakonia" (service) in the Christian Church, are usually younger men out of whose ranks the elders are frequently chosen.

THE PRESBYTERY

At the heart of the Presbyterian system stands the Presbytery. A Presbytery is composed of ministers and elders, each congregation being represented by at least one elder. Ordained ministers, who may be serving the Church within the territory covered by the Presbytery, whether as chaplains, teachers or secretaries of Church agencies, can also be members of the Presbytery. So, too, can ministers who have officially retired from the positions which they occupied.

In Presbyterianism the Presbytery occupies the position and exercises the authority which in Episcopacy is associated with the bishop. It was, in fact, created out of the context of primitive Christianity, in order to confront kings and prelates in the name of Christ, the Head of the Church. King James VI of Scotland, who succeeded Queen Elizabeth as James I of England, is alleged to have said that a Scottish Presbytery "agreeth as well with a monarchy as God and Devil." This was true, of course, only if monarchs overstepped the bounds of their authority and intervened in the affairs of the Church of Christ. The truth is that in the agitated period which followed the Reformation the "divine right of Presbytery" took the place of the "divine right of kings." In the seventeenth century, at the time when the Westminster Confession of Faith was being drafted, the "divine right of Presbytery" was maintained against Episcopalians on the one hand, and Independents on the other. It must be acknowledged, however, that due to the finitude and frailty of the best of humans, there has sometimes been truth in the criticism of John Milton, himself a theological Calvinist but an ecclesiastical Independent, that "New Presbyter is but old priest writ large." This remark has been seconded in our time by the Calvinist, Karl Barth.

The word "Presbytery" is Biblical. It occurs in the Greek New Testament as "Presbuterion," which was explained by Calvin to mean a "College of Presbyters." It represents committee or council government at its very best. It is government by consent, conciliar administration, in which all the parties concerned are represented. With all deference to Milton and Barth, and recognizing that there is no form of Church structure which is perfect in all its workings, this should be said. Presbyterian order, as centered in Presbyteries, is as close as the Church Universal has been able to come to the spirit and form of the Apostolic Church. It is, moreover, as adequate and creative a form as has yet emerged for the conduct of the Church's work.

The functions of Presbytery are various. It approves candidates for the ministry. It later ordains them when they are duly qualified for office and after they have received a call to service. It is Presbytery which deals with all questions relating to the orthodoxy or moral behavior of a minister. In the Church of Scotland it is the responsibility of the Presbytery to conduct a periodic study of the affairs of all congregations. In the United States, however, where, as already indicated, there is a tradition of greater independency than in Scotland, the Presbytery intervenes only when its help is solicited by a congregation, or when there is clear evidence of serious internal trouble in congregational affairs. Presbyteries have the right to overture the General Assembly on any matter which, in their judgment, concerns the welfare or mission of the Church. All matters involving a change in the constitution of the Church must have the approval of the Presbyteries before such changes can become operative. In most Presbyterian churches such approval involves a two-thirds majority of the Presbyteries on doctrinal matters; but in some a three-fourths majority is required.

As regards corporate planning on the part of Presbyteries to promote the Kingdom of Christ within their bounds, it has become the policy of American Presbyterianism to appoint General Presbyters. These men are vested with authority to exercise a general superintendence over the establishment and development of new churches within Presbytery bounds, to recommend new projects, and to stand in a pastoral relationship to institutions which function under Presbytery auspices. It is natural that Presbyteries should vary greatly as to their size, their spirit, their outlook, their problems, and the frequency of their meetings. But in their general organization they vary very little. In every instance the Moderator is elected for one year and may be a clergyman or an elder.

THE SYNODS

Next in the hierarchical scale of judicatories comes the Synod, which is made up of a number of Presbyteries. In

American Presbyterianism Synod boundaries have tended to coincide with state boundaries. This, however, is by no means universal. In the future the traditional principle of demarcation may become less general than it is today. As to their composition, Synods are of two main types. Some, the larger Synods in particular, are organized on a representational basis; not all the members of the constituent members may attend but only a delegated quota from each Presbytery. Synods of the other type may be attended by all members of Presbytery who find it possible to be present at the annual gathering.

It has been said, and with a great deal of justification, that in the United States Presbyterian Synods have to a large extent become "fifth wheels," so far as creative action is concerned. Beyond dealing with cases which may be referred to them by Presbyteries for advice or judicial action, Synod meetings today have chiefly a twofold significance. They provide an admirable opportunity for the Boards and Agencies of the Church to make inspirational appeals in the interests of the causes that they represent. Some Synods, moreover, especially the delegated Synods, offer admirable educational facilities for the ministers and elders who attend. Workshops are organized for the discussion of important issues relating to Synod projects or to the witness of the Church in general. Such Synods take their work much more seriously, in the best Presbyterian tradition, than do others whose main features are social and inspirational in character. Practically all Synods sponsor special projects within their bounds. For the presentation and discussion of these the annual Synod meeting provides an admirable opportunity.

The most significant development that has taken place in recent decades in the organization and work of Synods has been the appointment of officers on a full-time basis, whose responsibility it is to carry on projects which a Synod sponsors or in which it may be interested. Many of these projects are directly related to the work of the Board of National Missions or the Board of Christian Education. Epoch-making in this connection is the emergence of the Synod-Executive. This officer is responsible partly to the Synod Council and partly to Church Boards, and more recently to the General Council of the denomination. This new type of officer possesses great power. He is the present-day successor of the old-time Superintendent who emerged in Scotland in the early days of Presbyterianism in that country. The Superintendent functioned during a certain period on the frontiers of the nation, possessing virtual Episcopal authority of a functional kind. After his suppression in the home country, the Superintendent reappeared in Presbyterian Mission fields abroad. The present writer was once the Superintendent of the Free Church of Scotland Mission in Peru. The emergence of Synod Executives in American Presbyterianism is a quite natural development. It is consonant with the genius of Presbyterian order, which is flexible and makes provision for officers who are made responsible for frontier tasks and are vested with the requisite authority to carry them through. This is a respect in which American Presbyterianism has shown itself to be more dynamic and adventurous, and at the same time truer to the Presbyterian principle of adjusting structure to life, than has been the case in the Presbyterian Churches of Scotland in the post-Knox period. Scottish Presbyterianism has shown a consistent dread of vesting too much authority in the hands of any one individual. Because of that fear, the development of the Church has sometimes suffered both at home and abroad.

So far as Synods are concerned, the greatest problem which confronts American Presbyterianism today is this. In very many instances Synod boundaries do not embrace a natural region. By a "natural region," I mean an area whose inhabitants feel that they belong together. The bond between them may be historical sentiment or geographical situation, common cultural problems, or similar forms of business or industry. Members of the laity are accustomed to meet together to discuss common secular problems. Very rarely, however, do the political boundaries of a state enclose a natural region in this sense.

It is little less than tragic that the traditional boundaries of Presbyterian Synods do not correspond to the frontiers of important "natural regions." Take one instance, that of Metropolitan New York. This crucial region embraces virtually the whole area from Poughkeepsie, eighty miles up the Hudson, to Bridgeport, Connecticut, sixty miles to the Northeast, and reaches to Trenton on the Delaware River, sixty miles to the South. The Port of New York Authority now possesses jurisdiction over shipping on both the New York and Jersey sides of the Hudson. "The Children of this World" have in this instance made a more creative approach to their problem than "the Children of Light." So far as the Presbyterian approach to this great natural region is concerned, it is made by three distinct Synods, the Synod of New York, the Synod of New England and the Synod of New Jersey. These do not coordinate their activities. The result is that the tremendous common problems of people who belong together, whether they live on farms or in suburbia, in the inner or the outer city, are simply not dealt with by a great Church. The same is true of the important areas that surround Philadelphia and Pittsburgh. In each instance three different Presbyterian Synods deal with the affairs of people who live together in a natural region. Regional Synods are a supreme creative necessity in American Presbyterianism. A project to create such Synods across the nation was endorsed some years ago by more than two-thirds of the Presbyteries of the Presbyterian Church U.S.A. The time is ripe in the nation and in the Church for resurrecting an archived vision and translating it into regional reality from the Atlantic to the Pacific, from the Canadian to the Mexican border. Here is a situation in which the "Presbyterian Way" of today must break with mere traditionalism and vested interests and discover the highway to Tomorrow.

THE GENERAL ASSEMBLY

The great week in the Presbyterian year is General Assembly Week, when the supreme judicatory of the Church assembles for its annual meeting. The Church of Scotland General Assembly meets invariably in the historic city of Edinburgh where the Reformation took place under John Knox. In Western lands, however, and on the great frontiers of the Presbyterian world in Asia, Africa and Australia, the place of meeting of a General Assembly changes from year to year, from biennium to biennium, or quadrennium to quadrennium, as the case may be. Most General Assemblies of the Southern Presbyterian Church have convened at Montreat in the mountains of North Carolina, where the Church has the advantage of owning a remarkable set of buildings capable of providing Assembly members with facilities for both public sessions and personal entertainment. Its sister church, however, now the United Presbyterian Church in the U.S.A. since the Union of 1958, has traditionally been a pilgrim so far as concerns the rendezvous of its Annual Assembly. One-year Commissioners may find themselves in Philadelphia, where the first Presbyterian General Assembly was organized in 1789; their successors, the year following, may come together in Los Angeles, where the largest of the Church's two hundred and one Presbyteries has its seat.

But wherever the Assembly is held, the experience of being present at its sessions, whether as an official delegate representing a Presbytery, or as a corresponding member representing an Assembly Board or Agency, or simply as a visitor, is usually overwhelming. Clergy and laity, who have been appointed as Commissioners by the Presbyteries to which they belong, are there in equal numbers. Each Presbytery is given its quota according to its size. The total number of Commissioners exceeds a thousand men and women. Apart from the full-time officers of the Assembly and the leading officials of the Boards and Agencies of the denomination, who are invariably present to make reports and for consultation, but without vote, the composition of each General Assembly is totally different from every other. A Presbytery, of course, has the right to send the same person to successive Assemblies, but this is rarely done and only for some very special reason. Not even former Moderators are continuing members of Assembly, as they are in Scotland. Every effort is made to secure that each General Assembly shall be free and independent in making its decisions and not subject to pressures from any quarter. Communications addressed to members of the Assembly, after their election by pressure groups interested in some particular action being taken, are not infrequent; but they are not looked upon with favor.

For some two days before an Assembly convenes a Pre-Assembly Conference is held, at which addresses are given on Evangelism or some important aspect of the Church's mission. Many hundreds of visitors, as well as a goodly number of Commissioners, attend this gathering. Later, while the Assembly is in session, early morning breakfasts, special luncheons or dinners, as well as popular evening meetings in the Assembly Hall, are concomitant features of each annual gathering. Attendance at these special, unofficial functions has proved to be a profound spiritual experience for thousands of people. They have been confronted by outstanding speakers with phases of human need or illustrations of the saving power of Christ.

The Assembly is officially opened by a service of worship, at which time the retiring Moderator preaches a sermon. At the close of the sermon the Sacrament of the Lord's Supper is celebrated. Elders from local churches, moving with rhythmic reverence which has become famous, distribute the symbols of Christ's broken body and shed blood to the large multitude that throngs the place of meeting.

In the afternoon a new Moderator is elected. No one knows beforehand who will be the Assembly's choice. For in American Presbyterianism no official church committee chooses a nominee, as the traditional custom has been in Scotland, where the name of the future Moderator is announced six months in advance and the name chosen is merely presented to the Assembly for validation. Out of two, three, or even four persons nominated and seconded, with accompanying speeches, and subsequently voted upon by secret ballot, the leader of the Church for the ensuing year is duly elected and installed into office. There might be a more august and simpler way of Moderatorial election, but none that is more truly democratic, or more symbolical of a rooted horror in American Presbyterianism of being subject to the dictation or control of an ecclesiastical machine.

In the fulfillment of his duties as a presiding officer, the Moderator can count upon the guidance of the Stated Clerk of the General Assembly. This officer is the Church's chief authority on Presbyterian Law and on the proper conduct of Assembly business and debate. While Moderators come and go, the Stated Clerk remains. While it cannot be said that a Stated Clerk of a Presbyterian General Assembly is in any sense the chief administrative or executive officer of the Church, inasmuch as in Presbyterianism such an officer does not exist, it can be affirmed that, under all ordinary circumstances, the incumbent of this office is usually the most representative and influential figure in the denomination.

The work of the General Assembly is principally taken up in hearing and discussing reports from the Boards and Agencies of the Church, which function under the jurisdiction of the Assembly, and from other committees and commissions which the Assembly itself has appointed. Representatives from other churches and Christian bodies are welcomed from time to time by the Moderator and are given the privilege of addressing the Assembly. Year by year the most impressive single episode of the Assembly is when men and women from the younger churches overseas, together with missionary and fraternal workers who labor at their side on the frontiers of the Church Universal, appear on the platform as a single massive group. The most awesome moment in the life of an Assembly is the occasion when, with doors closed and all movement forbidden, the Permanent Judicial Commission makes its report. This Commission, which always includes some distinguished members of the legal profession, pronounces the final word on cases which have been appealed to it for judgment.

While the General Assembly of the world's largest Presbyterian Church does not have, as has been already stated, the degree of ecclesiastical authority that belongs, for example, to the Church of Scotland Assembly, its authority is very great indeed. It will be of interest to know wherein this authority consists.

According to the Constitution of the United Presbyterian Church, "The General Assembly shall receive all appeals, complaints and references that affect the doctrine or the interpretation of the Constitution of the Church, that are regularly brought before it from the lower judicatories, and having first decided that a question of doctrine of the interpretation of the Constitution of the Church is involved, shall decide the case.

"To the General Assembly also belongs the power of deciding in all controversies respecting doctrine and the interpretation of the Constitution of the Church; of reporting, warning, or bearing testimony against error in doctrine or immorality in practice in any Church, Presbytery or Synod; of erecting new Synods and of dividing, uniting or otherwise combining Synods, or portions of Synods previously existing, and approving the union, division or erecting of Presbyteries by Synods; of authorizing a Synod or a Presbytery to receive under its jurisdiction a body suited to become a constituent part of said judicatory and lying within its geographical bounds; of uniting with other ecclesiastical bodies, such union to be effected by the mode of procedure defined in this form of government; of superintending the concerns of the whole Church; of corresponding with other churches, on such terms as may be agreed upon by the General Assembly and the corresponding body; of suppressing schismatical contentions and disputations; and in general of recommending and attempting reformation of manners, and the promotion of charity, truth and holiness, through all the churches under its care."

At the time of the recent Church Union there was added to this traditional article the following sentence: "The General Assembly, being the supreme judicial, legislative and administrative court of the Church, may deal with and dispose of any matter which may arise, and which is not provided for in the Constitution or rules of the Church or its forms of procedure."

Already this new provision has come under attack. It is argued that it invests the General Assembly with an authority which was never delegated to it by Presbyteries. It could conduce to an undesirable degree of centrality action in the administration of the Church. In conceivable circumstances it could lead to grave disunity in the Church. Fearing that "the final sentence of this Section might be construed as changing the characteristic form of our Church government from one in which the Presbytery has inherent power to one in which the General Assembly might become a centralized and undelegated ecclesiastical power," the Standing Committee on Polity of the 1959 General Assembly was authorized to send down this matter for the consideration and decision of the Presbyteries. By action of the General Assembly of 1960 the offending sentence was eliminated.

While this traditional fear of undue centralization of authority needs to be taken seriously, a tribute must be paid to the remarkable transformation through which the Presbyterian Church in the U.S.A. passed, from the viewpoint of organizational efficiency, during the decade before it merged with its sister Church, the United Presbyterian Church of North America. The General Council of the General Assembly was formerly a small, unrepresentative body, appointed by the Assembly, very largely for the purpose of mediating between the powerful Boards and Agencies of the Church in order to determine how much financial support each should receive. It became transformed into a large, representative, dynamic body which was given authority to develop policies for the Church as a whole. The Council, after its reorganization, was given a permanent staff under the leadership of a full-time Secretary. It has since assumed certain administrative responsibilities in relation to some areas of the Church's work. The Secretary maintains close contact with Synod Executives who, on their several fields, coordinate the work of the Boards and Agencies. The perennial problem might be stated thus: How shall a great denomination provide for itself dynamic leadership in such a way that organizational structure shall not violate the freedom which is the birthright of individuals and judicatories, but shall always be the servant of clear vision and dedicated energies, under the direction of the Holy Spirit?

I close this chapter with the same thought with which I began. *The structure of the Church is for the life of the Church.*

✣ **7** ✣

Presbyterians at Worship

IN ONE of the greatest passages in world literature the German writer Goethe puts these words into the mouth of one of his characters: "One thing there is which no child brings into the world with him; and yet it is on this one thing that all depends for making him in every point a man—Reverence."

Supreme, according to Goethe, among the three forms of reverence, which a true man must attain, is reverence for "what is above him." The reverence which leads him to look upwards is the source of the other two reverences: reverence for what is around him, and reverence for what is beneath him. What the great humanist was feeling after, if not actually suggesting, is this: The achievement of humanity worthy of the name is the fruit of religious worship. To be in the truest sense a man's man, sympathetically interested in one's coequals and passionately concerned about those less fortunate than one's self, a man must "lift up his eyes to the hills;" he must worship God.

But what does it mean to worship God in a Christian sense? In the "upward look," which marks all worship, there must be a creative awareness of God, a true knowledge of God and a sincere aspiration after God. True worship must also be accompanied by dutiful obedience to God, which is something quite different from engaging in religious exercises, simple or complex, or indulging in moralistic behavior. In the Old Testament the worship of God and the service of God are practically synonymous terms. Worship is inseparable from service. This is made particularly plain in the writings of the Prophets where the worshiper passes beyond rites and ceremonies into the spiritual service of God. This is still more true in the New Testament. While to "worship the Father in spirit and truth" need not exclude ceremonial, the latter is not of the essence of worship.

The true significance of Christian worship has lingered on in the phrase "Divine Service." Worship, whatever its accompaniments, must be adoring and obedient love to God, together with the loving service of one's neighbor as God's child. The indissoluble relationship between worship and service, between adoring love and loving obedience, in the New Testament, receives classical expression in Paul's Letter to the Romans. In the King James Version the famous passage in Chapter 12, verse 1, is rendered thus: "I beseech you, therefore, brethren, by the mercies of God, that you present your bodies a living sacrifice, holy, acceptable unto God, *which is your reasonable service.*" The Revised Standard Version, with truer sensitivity to the Greek original, changes the phrase "your reasonable service" into "*your spiritual worship.*"

One of the objectives of the Protestant Reformation was, as has been well expressed, to remove from Christian worship "all medieval and sacerdotal accretions in order to achieve the simplicity and purity of the primitive rites." Luther and Calvin were equally interested in this restoration. Both raised the question of the authority for this or that form of worship; both were eager to provide for the participation of the laity in the services of the sanctuary; both were agreed that worship must express itself in life. Whereas Luther, however, believed that the formal patterns for worship were not prescribed in the Bible, Calvin held that the Bible was also authoritative in all matters relating to the public worship of God. Thus it came about that Calvin and all whom he inspired, the English Puritans in particular, developed a concern regarding Biblical authority for forms of worship. They wanted to be sure that God was worshiped in the way in which He wanted to be worshiped. Worship must, therefore, conform to the Word of God. For that reason "purity of worship" has been a major concern in Presbyterian history. An equal concern has been the adaptation of forms of worship to the condition of the worshiper.

THE PUBLIC WORSHIP OF GOD

In recent times the Christian churches in the West, both Protestant and Roman Catholic, have shown a reawakened interest in the subject of public worship. A veritable liturgical movement has swept the churches. This does not necessarily mean a resurgence of ritualistic practices in the medieval sense, although aberrations in this direction are witnessed from time to time. It does mean, however, that the question is up afresh as to how "*liturgia*," "public worship," can be made worthy in the highest degree of the God who is worshiped, and at the same time most spiritually helpful to those who take part in the worship service. Presbyterians have become deeply involved in this reborn concern.

It is important, before we consider the present-day situation and trends as regards worship in Presbyterian Churches, that I should briefly describe the characteristics of Presbyterian worship from the days of Calvin and Knox.

It was the passionate desire of both those great men to restore and preserve the Catholic, New Testament tradition of worship. This they sought to do in loyal, lowly subjection to the authority and centrality of the Word. The genius of the form of worship which they sponsored was inspired by a feeling of reverent awe and abasement before the majesty of the living God. The worshipers were intensely aware of God's greatness and their own nothingness. They, therefore, took up in His presence the attitude of willing and obedient servants. Overwhelmingly conscious of the fact that they owed everything to God, Who had freed them from the bondage of sin and adopted them into this family through Jesus Christ, they desired to lay their all at his feet for his service.

There was consequently a certain somberness in Reformed worship. Everything was excluded that did not appear to have the sanction of the Word. In contrast to this, Lutheran worship, in consonance with the characteristic subjectivity of the Lutheran mood, was a buoyant expression of gratitude to God for His grace and mercy. Its manifestation was not trammeled by the question whether it had New Testament sanction for its pattern. It burst forth exuberantly in hymns of the new life, soon to be accompanied by the sonorous strains of the organ. In Reformed and Presbyterian Churches, on the other hand, the Psalms of David, unaccompanied by instrumental music, constituted the sole book of praise for many generations on the European Continent, in Great Britain and America. With respect to the conduct of worship, moreover, the whole stress was laid upon the use of the lips and the ear. The Word was spoken and sung and heard; God was addressed in prayer and in praise. But, where the Word occupied the supreme and exclusive place in worship, nothing relating to the eye had any participation whatever.

The question came up very early whether the form of worship should be liturgical or free. Should the minister make use of set forms of prayer, or should he be free to use extempore prayer? It is a highly significant fact that the English speaking congregation in Geneva, of which John Knox was pastor during the years of his exile from Scotland, used a simple book of worship called *The Form of Prayers*. This service book was used in the Church of Scotland for a hundred years, under the name of *The Book of Common Order*. When that Scottish lady, Jeannie Geddes, flung her stool at the head of a preacher in the old Church of St. Giles, Edinburgh, the reason for her action and for the riot that ensued was not that the minister read his prayers from a book. The congregation of St. Giles was not unused to liturgical worship. The cause of the uproar was that he used the Prayer Book of the Church of England, which was being imposed upon the Church of

Scotland without the consent of the people. Subsequently, due to the influence of the Puritans, who desired to restore to the Church a more prophetic conception of worship, and who were prejudiced against liturgy in every form, because they wanted to give maximum participation to the people, free worship took the place of liturgical worship in the churches of Scotland. This tradition continued until early in the present century, when the use of liturgical forms was made optional.

The practice of free worship, with extempore prayer, which has become a characteristic of Presbyterian Church services for more than two centuries, both in Great Britain and the United States, was not the result of unreasoning prejudice. It was grounded in the conviction that in public worship God should be given a chance to breathe His Holy Spirit upon the minister. The minister, on his part, under the inspiration of the Spirit, and drawing upon his personal knowledge as the shepherd of a flock, should in his prayers give vocal expression to the deepest needs and aspirations of the congregation.

Here is something which merits consideration in the new liturgical era. Nothing is more moving, more impressive and more worshipful than extempore prayer at its best. When the pastor steeps his soul in God's truth and his people's needs, when he is sensitive to happenings in his neighborhood and the world, when he prepares carefully his heart and mind before representing his people at God's "Throne of Grace," there is nothing in liturgy that can equal the voice of free prayer. Because a prayer is "extempore," it does not mean that it is uttered without due preparation or that it need be slovenly or trite. It can be all these, of course, and has frequently been so; but "free" prayer should not, and need not, be trite or slovenly or unworshipful. Indeed, I have no hesitation in saying that "Free Worship" when worthily conducted, the minister being what he ought to be and having prepared himself adequately for the worship service, expresses Presbyterian worship at its historical best. It is truest also to its classical understanding of man's approach to Deity. It must be frankly acknowledged, moreover, that under certain circumstances, liturgical worship can become depressingly reactionary. It can even degenerate into a dull, soulless religiosity. Not only so, but in many instances the development of an elaborate ritual, with all manner of aesthetic adjuncts in sound and color, becomes a substitute for the spiritual worship of God. So far as a certain type of minister is concerned, it offers an escape from the necessity of unveiling an inward shallowness, and becomes a mask for the absence of a deeply religious spirit.

Having said this, however, and having made clear my personal predilection for non-liturgical worship at its best, I hasten to emphasize the fact that the free and unimposed use of liturgy is by no means alien to Presbyterian worship. Not only so, but the reawakened interest in liturgical practice which marks Presbyterianism today in the United States, and in many other parts of the world, is healthful and can be creative in the service of God and in the mission of the Church.

Early in the present century, under the inspiration of the famous Princeton University professor, Henry van Dyke, a layman, who had won distinction for himself in the fields of letters and diplomacy, there was organized *The Church Service Society*. Its design was to stimulate interest in a worthier form of divine worship in Presbyterian sanctuaries. I can recall the impression made upon me personally by the exceeding drabness of the worship services held in Princeton Seminary, Presbyterianism's leading theological institution, when I arrived on the campus as a student in 1913. A complete break had taken place with the earlier days of Presbyterianism in Scotland and the United States. In those days the minister in the pulpit had something distinctive above his garb. But now there was no white tie, no special collar, no gown, no white bands, no old-time precentor to lead the praise, and, of course, no choir. I carried away memories of impressive things I heard spoken, but there was nothing in the service that created a true sense of corporate worship. The head was instructed but the heart was left unmoved. One thing that was particularly lacking was a sense of the Church. A worshiper had the feeling of being a mere individual with no sense of belonging to a fellowship.

In less than a half century all has changed. There has taken place a restoration of Reformed worship in Presbyterian churches throughout the nation. The traditional ideal of Presbyterian worship, that of spontaneity within the context of an ordered framework, was transfigured and given literary expression in *The Book of Common Worship*. The Church rediscovered its own heritage of worship and the heritage of the Church Universal. This rediscovery and restoration coincided with a reborn sense of Christ's Church as a corporate reality, locally and throughout the globe. A new churchliness came into being, and with it an awareness that God had created the eye as well as the ear and the lips. While vestments, collars, bands, the Celtic cross, stained glass windows, more churchly architecture and the optional use of liturgy can, of course, become ends in themselves and substitutes for true Christian worship, which must always be "in spirit and in truth," nevertheless, the spirit and direction of the present liturgical movement within Presbyterianism is wholesome. This is said by one who, both theologically and by temperament, has an intense dislike for mere ritual as such. For that reason I rejoice that there has been no disposition anywhere in Presbyterian circles to regard liturgical practice as being of the very essence of Christian worship, nor any disposition to make mandatory the use of a particular pattern of worship. A repetition of the famous Jeannie Geddes incident is exceedingly unlikely in contemporary Presbyterianism.

Let me close this section, therefore, by quoting from the two Presbyterian classics in the realm of liturgy which have been published in recent times by Scottish and American Presbyterians respectively. Both make clear that freedom in the form of public worship must ever be a part of the "Presbyterian Way."

In the preface to *The Book of Common Order*, published by the reunited Church of Scotland in 1940, we read these words: "Liberty in the conduct of worship is a possession which the Church of Scotland will not surrender. But a service book is necessary to express the mind of the Church with regard to its offices of worship, in orders and forms which, while not fettering individual judgment in particulars, will set the norm for the orderly and reverent conduct of the various public services in which ministers have to lead their people."

In 1944 the General Assembly of the Presbyterian Church in the U.S.A. approved the publication of *The Book of Common Worship*. It had been prepared by a special committee on the basis of previous volumes bearing the same title and associated with the name of Henry van Dyke. The Preface to this book, which is now in use in the United Presbyterian Church in the U.S.A., contains these significant paragraphs: "The customs and teachings concerning worship prevailing under the leadership of the Reformers, together with the direction given by the Westminster Divines, have been rediscovered and are profoundly influencing discussions now going on. Your Committee has carefully followed this movement and those who know intimately the worship and doctrines of the Reformed faith will find that the forms and orders in this book express faithfully the standards of our Church.

"A second movement that has influenced the Committee is the revival of interest in Christian worship. This revival is common to all the churches. Our Presbyterian Church has always emphasized its liberty and has left its ministers free as to the form and order of worship. This freedom, however, has often resulted in worship as formal and as forced as a prepared liturgy. The movement within the Church looking to the improvement of worship seeks, therefore, not only to provide the minister with the treasures in thought and expression that are the inheritance of the Church, but to encourage Christian congregations to more active participation in Christian worship, which was the custom of the early Church and is the heritage of the Protestant Reformation."

THE PREACHING OF THE WORD

For Presbyterians the center and culmination of a regular Sunday service is the sermon. A true sermon is, in the Reformed tradition, the proclamation of the Word of God. Through a human mouthpiece God literally communicates His truth, as through the Prophets and Apostles of olden time, but with this difference. The truth proclaimed by a minister of the Word of God does not add new truth to that which was revealed through the Apostles and Prophets and which became Incarnate in Jesus Christ, who is the Eternal Word of God. In genuine preaching, however, that is, in preaching as it should be and can be when the preacher subjects himself to the Word of God, the sermon sheds light upon some phase of the everlasting truth and applies it with spiritual warmth to the actual needs of those who listen. Deeply enshrined in the Presbyterian tradition of worship is the conviction that in the sermon, when lips anointed by the Spirit speak to ears attuned to the Spirit, the very Voice of God is heard. It is understandable, therefore, that in this tradition the Christian minister fulfills a permanently prophetic function. Neither an impressive ritualistic ceremony nor a homily replete with practical admonition can take the place of a sermon. Only in a secondary sense, and in the sense in which the term can be applied to all true Christians, is the Presbyterian minister a "priest."

The soul of all preaching is, of course, the Gospel, which is the central core of the Word of God. The minister of the Word is supremely and inescapably a "minister of the Gospel." Preaching is never expressive of what Presbyterianism has conceived to be indispensable unless, somehow, somewhere, every sermon is illumined by the saving knowledge of God. In every sermonic utterance the preacher should make unmistakably plain how God may be known savingly, and what is the relationship of such saving knowledge to the particular phase or facet of truth with which he has been dealing. This means that bathed in evangelical light, and conveyed with evangelistic warmth, an appropriate, fresh, unhackneyed allusion to "Jesus Christ, the Son of God, the Saviour," should find a place in every sermon, whatever the theme, the occasion, or the place. How to do this in a vital manner, making use of all the resources of literature and art, of experience and history, is one of the abiding tasks of the science of Homiletics. To provide reasons why this should be done, why the Saviourhood of Jesus Christ, God's Son, the Bible's central theme, the Church's sovereign Lord, should be unfailingly sounded or glimpsed in every message of every preacher, is one of the abiding tasks of theology. It was an Anglican, William Temple, the late Archbishop of Canterbury, a man whose theology was in the best Reformed tradition, who said in the famous Jerusalem Statement of 1928, "Our Message is Jesus Christ."

The length of a Presbyterian sermon in those early days in the Scottish Highlands, when I was a boy, was one hour. It could not fail to be didactic, as it was supposed to be, and was often excessively so. There were some ministers who specialized as "Law" preachers. They felt called of God to stab the hearts of their hearers with sharp arrows of truth which were barbed with divine imperatives. Their design was to awake the slumbering lost to their peril and responsibility, and to wound their consciences that they might become aware of their need. Others were known as specialists in "Gospel" preaching. Their words came as a balsam for spirits that had been wounded by the Law. There were others, and they have constituted the majority in Presbyterian pulpits, in whose preaching arrows have sped from the bow and oil has been poured from the cruse.

This is the true ideal for all Christian preaching. Apart from the Law, the Gospel cannot be understood or be more than mere sentimentalism. Apart from the Gospel the Law cannot escape becoming pure moralism. The preacher in whom the sense of mission is intense appears before his people in the spirit of Thomas Chalmers, with a due sensitivity to the dimensions of Time and Eternity. He preaches "as a dying man to dying men." This by no means signifies, either for preacher or hearer, a morbid apprehension of Death; it does mean for all concerned a redemptive recognition of the importance of Life and of fulfilling one's life mission "while it is day." It means also that preaching is for a verdict. The sermon as the climactic point in Reformed worship is not to be judged by its magnificence as a pulpit display, or by the entertainment, even the devout entertainment it provides for those who occupy the pews, but rather by the measure in which preacher and people leave the sanctuary in a state of dedicated response to the Word of God.

Many things have combined to give the preaching service of today, in Presbyterian as in other churches, a very changed character from what it had in the days before this rushing, technological era. The Presbyterian tradition for sermon-making was careful preparation, the commitment of thought to writing in the form of a complete manuscript, or very full notes, with the subsequent free delivery of the discourse. Today when the sermon is no longer governed by the falling sand in an hourglass, but varies from twenty to thirty minutes in length, the average Presbyterian preacher keeps close to his manuscript, even when he does not actually read the written text. Some memorize the manuscript, others visualize the pages. Still others take to the pulpit a structure of thought, the logical sequence of which they have mentally or with their pen clothed with words and images. Then leaving themselves to the Spirit's guidance, and sensitive to their environment, they preach the Word. This is the type of preaching most consonant with the Presbyterian heritage in the practice of Homiletics. It is also the most effective type, though by far the most difficult in which to achieve excellence. But when excellence is achieved, the sermon thus delivered literally sings itself into the hearts of the hearers. The mere reading of a sermon from the pulpit makes it difficult to create that singing note which the proclamation of truth, and especially of Christian truth, should have.

But whether or not the thought in which the Word of God

is proclaimed from the pulpit has a lilt to it, the present-day Presbyterian preacher delivers his sermon in an atmosphere that has richly re-echoed to the strains of melody and to the rhythmic cadences of responsive reading. It was one of the glories of the earliest Presbyterian witness to restore the people's participation in worship which had been lost in the Medieval period. First, it was the congregational singing of the Hebrew Psalms reduced to meter. Then came the singing of metrical paraphrases of the Bible and later of hymns written by devout, poetic souls. In time the sonorous strains of the organ, with accompanying choirs; the recitation of the Lord's Prayer and the Apostles' Creed; the reading of selected Scripture passages responsively or in unison by all the people, increased congregational participation in worship and prepared the hearts of the worshipers for worship's culminating act, the preaching of the Word.

More and more the buildings in which Presbyterians worship God and listen to the Word preached have an aesthetic quality which they lacked in the early days. At that time a sense of God's presence was so overwhelmingly real that the worshipers felt no need of anything in architectural form or sensuous symbol to create a sense of the Eternal Presence. Is the total setting for the preaching of the Word more spiritual and worthy today than it was yesterday? In a time when liturgy is renascent and the architectural design of Christian sanctuaries is replete with symbols and awesome in magnificence, it is important that Presbyterians and all Christians remember the words of Christianity's greatest preacher, "He dwelleth not in temples made with hands." It is not un-Presbyterian, but is in classical accord with the "Presbyterian Way," to establish for all preaching the criterion which I am about to suggest, and to apply it in the full awareness that the aesthetic setting in which the Word of God is preached is always relative and unessential and can be totally irrelevant. The criterion is this: Does the light that streams through windows rich in color and adorned with art fall upon faces that are anxiously looking for the truth and do not find it? It is fitting that we who are Presbyterian ministers of the Word, each time we preach in a gorgeous sanctuary, should remember the words of the poet Milton and search our hearts in their light.

"The hungry sheep look up and are not fed."

Happily, however, it is not of the genius of Presbyterianism to link the preaching of the Word to any holy place, whether its form be Gothic or Colonial, or just a plain hall. The most memorable sermons ever preached by Presbyterian ministers were delivered in the open air or in meeting halls. Famous in the Scottish tradition is the grassy amphitheater by the Burn of Ferintosh in Ross shire where ten thousand worshipers used to gather at the "Communion Season." More famous still is a field in the Kirk of Shotts in Lanarkshire where on a Monday morning in the seventeenth century, five hundred people were converted as a result of a single sermon preached by a young minister, John Livingstone. This estimate was based on a careful survey which was made several years later. And what shall we say of the sacred spots among the hills of Southern Scotland where the persecuted Covenanters held their Conventicles?

Enshrined in the tradition of American Presbyterianism is the great meeting hall in Montreat, North Carolina, and the corresponding hall in Northfield, Massachusetts, the home center of Dwight L. Moody. In recent decades scores of meeting places and camping centers dedicated to spiritual objectives have come into being throughout the States of the Union. In those centers all manner of groups assemble in the summer months for the study of their faith in relation to life, to worship God together and to listen to the proclamation of the Word. At the present time, there is in process of development, in the Arizona plateau, a striking project called Ghost Ranch. To that place, midst a countryside similar to that where the "Word of God Incarnate" began His ministry, Faith and Life, the Word and the Sacraments, resort from time to time.

It is not by chance that the genius of Presbyterianism for

services of worship in the heart of nature, and for evangelism conducted beyond the bounds of the sanctuary should have produced a number of significant names in evangelistic history during the past hundred years. A Presbyterian layman, Duncan Matheson, was the soul of a great revival movement in Scotland in the mid-nineteenth century. Another Scottish layman, the distinguished scientist, Henry Drummond, whose life was wholly written by his friend, the great orientalist, George Adam Smith, became world famous as an Evangelist in student circles. Imperishable in the annals of preaching is Drummond's sermon, "Love, the Greatest Thing in the World." Dwight L. Moody, Wilbur Chapman, Billy Sunday, men who made an impact in their time on the religious life of America were all Presbyterians. It can be said also that Billy Graham, that ecumenical Southern Baptist, has had no more loyal supporters in his evangelistic endeavors than Presbyterian clergymen in the great urban centers that he visited. These range from Tom Allan of Glasgow, Scotland, author of *The Face of My Parish,* to John Sutherland Bonnell, minister of the Fifth Avenue Presbyterian Church, New York.

THE ADMINSTRATION OF THE SACRAMENTS

In common with other Evangelical Christians, Presbyterians believe that Christ instituted two, and only two, Sacraments: Baptism and the Lord's Supper. These Sacraments, when administered, are "means of grace" and an integral part of the public worship of God. In the Westminster Confession of Faith, Sacraments are defined as follows: "Sacraments are holy signs and seals of the Covenant of grace, immediately instituted by God, to represent Christ and his benefits, and to confirm our interest in Him; as also to put a visible difference between those who belong unto the Church, and the rest of the world, and solemnly to engage them to the service of God in Christ, according to His Word." The meaning and implications of this conception of the Sacraments will become clear as we take them up individually.

BAPTISM

In many Presbyterian Churches the Sacrament of Baptism is administered once a month. On a given Sunday a group of parents with children in their arms, or by their side, stand before their minister. A Presbyterian minister has been ordained to be a "minister of the Word and Sacraments." The parents have already seen the minister in private. It is understood that at least one parent is a baptized Christian and so a member of the Visible Church. They are asked to acknowledge their faith in Christ as Saviour and Lord; they promise to be true Christian parents to their children; that they will pray with them and for them and bring them up "in the nurture and admonition of the Lord." They equally promise that, when their children come to years of discretion, they will "guide them to a personal profession of Jesus Christ as Saviour and Lord and into full Communion with the Church." In the course of a simple service, the minister, having briefly expounded the meaning of Baptism and engaged in prayer, sprinkles with water the forehead of each child, who is usually held by the father, saying at the same time and while the congregation reverently stands, "James—Helen—I baptize thee in the name of the Father, and of the Son, and of the Holy Ghost, Amen." He closes the service with the words, "The blessing of God Almighty, Father, Son and Holy Ghost, descend upon thee and dwell in thine heart forever."

When the Sacrament involves the Baptism of an adult who was not baptized as a child, the service becomes exceedingly impressive. The person to be baptized, having made a full profession of Christian faith, kneels down. He is then baptized by the sprinkling of water in the name of the Holy Trinity, while all those present reverently stand. The person thus baptized becomes a member of the Visible Church and is eligible for admission to full communicant status.

What does Baptism signify for Presbyterians? At the moment the whole quesion of Baptism is under discussion in the Reformed and Presbyterian Churches, with Karl Barth of Basel and Thomas Torrance of Edinburgh playing a leading part. To the question "What is Baptism?" the Westminster Catechism answers, "Baptism is a Sacrament, wherein the washing with water, in the name of the Father and of the Son and of the Holy Ghost, doth signify and seal our ingrafting into Christ, and partaking of the benefits of the Covenant of grace, and our engagement to be the Lord's."

Baptism is the symbolical ceremony of initiation into the Christian Church, which is the sphere where the grace of God operates in a special manner. The symbolism becomes most fully apparent when the baptized person is dipped in water. This act signifies spiritual renewal through his dying to sin, his rising with Christ from the dead, and his engagement to be the Lord's, whose name he bears. There is nothing indeed in the Presbyterian Standards that would forbid a minister to baptize an adult by immersion. The Confession of Faith states explicitly, however, and rightly, that "dipping of the person into the water is not necessary, but Baptism is rightly administered by pouring or sprinkling water upon the person." What is important is the element used, not its amount nor the form of its application. While for the baptized person, especially the adult, Baptism becomes a special means of grace, it does not involve spiritual regeneration, as is held by some Christians.

As regards the infant who is baptized, the Baptismal vows are taken by his parents. In this instance Baptism becomes in a special sense the dedication of the child to God. Its efficacy, therefore, will depend to a very large extent upon the seriousness with which parents fulfill their responsibility to lead their child little by little to a saving knowledge of God. This will mean a deeply devotional atmosphere in the home. It is most essential that the growing boy or girl witness in all family relations the reality of the Christian life and be attracted to it.

WORSHIP IN THE HOME

This leads me to pause in the sequence of our thought in order to say a word about family religion in the Presbyterian tradition. My earliest recollection of the home into which I was born is the memory of family worship. Morning and evening the Bible was read and parents and children knelt in prayer. Engraven in my spirit forever are the words which would break like a refrain into our evening hilarity, "Now children," my father would say, "it's time to take the Book." And the Book, or rather the Books, would be taken. After singing a Psalm together, all of us who could would read a couple of Bible verses in turn around the little circle, till the chapter came to an end. This scene, which was once practically universal in Presbyterian homes in Scotland and the Western World and which still lingers in many, has been immortalized in matchless verse by Robert Burns in his "Cotter's Saturday Night."

> The priest-like father reads the sacred page
> How Abram was the friend of God on high;
> Or Jobs' pathetic plaint and wailing cry
> Or rapt Isaiah's wild, seraphic fire.
>
> Perhaps the Christian volume is the theme,
> How guiltless blood for guilty man was shed;
> How He, who bore in Heav'n the second name,
> Had not on earth whereon to lay His head,
>
> Then kneeling down to Heaven's Eternal King
> The saint, the father, and the husband prays.

I have often thought that the full restoration of this old "Presbyterian Way" in contemporary America would transfigure the home. It would also provide classes for young communicants with a rich spiritual basis. Family worship at some hour of the day, or some day of the week, would do something else. It would provide parents with a sacred period when the members of the household could listen to God together as He speaks in the Book. In simple extempore petitions, or through the use of some manual of devotion such as "Today," or "The Upper Room," or one of many others, they could lisp to Him their desires. Tensions would be relieved, ominous silences would be broken. Light would have a chance to dispel some dismal gloom and Christ be free to enter as a hallowed guest. Home religion with family devotions is the supreme answer to the contemporary problem of broken homes. Communion with Christ must be cultivated by Christians in the home, or their participation in Holy Communion in the church will be but solemn mockery.

THE LORD'S SUPPER

We come finally to the climactic event in congregational life and Christian experience, namely, participation in the Sacrament of the Lord's Supper. I have said that for Presbyterians the sermon is climactic in public worship. That is ordinarily true, except on those occasions when the Community of Christ celebrates the Holy Ordinance in which the dying love of their Saviour is set forth under the symbols of bread and wine. On such occasions, which come four times in the year at least, the spoken proclamation of the Word becomes the established prelude to being nourished by the risen life of the Incarnate Word.

The Lord's Supper, Holy Communion, the Eucharist, whatever be the designation used to describe Christianity's most sacred ordinance, is much more than a commemorative ceremony as some Christians conceive it to be. On the other hand, it is not to be regarded as a dramatic spectacle whereby the death of Christ is re-enacted, so that at the command of a priest and under severe ecclesiastical control, the Risen Lord becomes afresh the "host," (*hostia*) that is, the "victim" who is crucified afresh. The Lord Christ is indeed the "Host" but at the Table, and in an active not a passive sense. To those who in faith come as guests to His Table in response to the command, "This do in remembrance of Me," and who, discerning the Lord's body, "eat of the bread and drink of the cup," the

Risen one who is "alive forevermore" literally communicates His life.

Presbyterians have always emphasized the Real Presence in the Sacrament of the Lord's Supper. The material elements of bread and wine remain unchanged. But the living Lord so communicates to His people His actual, though invisible Selfhood, that they become partakers of His very being, for "their spiritual nourishment and growth in grace." For this Sacrament is designed for their inner renewal and for their upbuilding as members of Christ's Body, the Church. The late lamented Dr. Donald Baillie of St. Andrews movingly expresses, and in terms of the central Presbyterian tradition, the abiding meaning and implications of the Lord's Supper. In a special paper prepared for a Conference on "Faith and Order" he wrote, "The Living Lord gives Himself to be known to us within the actual ongoing Church and nowhere else. . . . He cannot be holden in the fixity of the past. In other words, the Eucharist means the enactment of the Living Christ today, and every day it is celebrated."

This is most important for an understanding of the Presbyterian view of the Lord's Supper. Christ Jesus, being both Saviour and Lord, supplies those who are guests at His Table, not only with spiritual energy for their ongoing needs, but also with special guidance and strength to meet the historic situation in which their lot is cast. It was because he believed so profoundly in the centrality of the Lord's Supper in the life of the Church that Calvin favored its celebration in the several congregations each Lord's Day morning. He was forced, however, to bow to other influences; and for the sake of the unity of the Church he accepted the pattern of less frequency which commended itself to his brethren.

So central in Presbyterianism has been the "Communion," as it has been familiarly called in Scotland, that during the seventeenth, eighteenth, and nineteenth centuries it was the apex of a gathering which lasted five days in all. The "Communion Season," which was an annual or biennial occasion, began on a Thursday, which was the "Fast Day." On this day regular Church services were held as on a Sunday. Friday was the "Men's Day." During this day the "men," that is, those regarded as having special stature in the Christian life, would "speak to the Question." The "Question" was some spiritual issue, usually involving Christian experience and the marks of the true believer. It would be propounded by one of the "men," and spoken to by a large number of others while the congregation listened. The discussion was always summed up by the minister who would add his own comments. Saturday was "Preparation Day." At the close of the morning service, Communion "tokens" were given out to prospective communicants. Others who might desire to become communicant members for the first time were given an opportunity to appear before the Session.

"Communion Sunday" was opened by a seven o'clock prayer meeting led by the "men." The regular worship service, which in the Northern territory would be held in the open air and attended by many hundreds and even thousands of people, could last from 11 A.M. to 5 P.M. The hour sermon was followed by the "Fencing of the Tables." At that time the presiding minister would make clear who had a right to sit down at the "Lord's Table," and who had not. Then the "Tables," at least three in succession, would begin to be served. The improvised communion tables, all covered with white cloths, with seats for communicants provided on both sides, would occupy an area in front of the "Tent," or wooden pulpit. While verses of the One Hundred and Third Psalm were being sung, the communicants would file into their places. After the "tokens" had been collected, the presiding minister would give a brief address and proceed to administer the Sacrament, the elements being then distributed by the elders. The "Table Service" concluded with a brief admonition to those communicating, after which they returned to their place, to the singing of the same famous Communion Psalm. Another "Table" would follow in the same manner, and yet another, each lasting approximately one hour. The "Communion Season" originally terminated with the Sunday services. In memory, however, of the famous Kirk of Shotts Communion, already referred to, at which five hundred people were converted, Monday was added as a day of Thanksgiving, during which a regular preaching service was also held. The great company thereafter dispersed on foot or in cart or buggy.

The times have changed. So, too, have certain adjuncts of a Presbyterian Communion. In most churches today there is a preparatory week-day service before the Sunday when the Sacrament is "celebrated." Communicant classes have been going on in the congregation for weeks. After the sermon on Sunday morning, the minister takes his place behind the Communion Table. The Table upon which are laid the sacred elements is covered with a white cloth. The cloth is removed during the singing of a hymn. Seated near the minister or standing on either side of him are the elders, while the members of the congregation occupy their regular pews. In Scotland a large number of the central pews are also covered with white cloths. After the minister has followed one of the forms of service suggested in the "Book of Common Worship," with appropriate prayer and singing, the Bread and the Wine are "set apart for that holy use for which Christ has ordained them." The elements are then given into the hands of the elders who distribute them first to the minister or ministers and thereafter to the people. After the congregation has been served in their pews, the Bread and the Cup are given by the minister to the officiating elders who in the meantime have resumed their seats. During the singing of a closing hymn, the elements on the Table are again covered by two of the elders with the same white cloth. The Benediction is pronounced and the Communion Service is over.

Some concluding observations may set the Communion Service in perspective as it is conducted in Presbyterian churches. Two considerations are never absent. *First,* participation in the Lord's Supper is for those, and for those only, who sincerely love Jesus Christ, who have made a public profession of faith in Christ and whose lives are consistent with their profession. *Second,* for Presbyterians, the Lord's Table is in the strictest sense the Table of the *Lord*. It is not the Table of any one congregation, denomination or ecclesiastical body. Christ is the Host. For that reason it has always been the practice of Presbyterians, who have not fallen into sectarian ways and so denied their own tradition, to invite to participate in the Sacrament of the Lord's Supper any professing Christian who happens to be in the congregation, whatever be the church to which he may belong. It is natural, therefore, that open Communion should be one of the basic tenets of Presbyterianism. For that reason Presbyterians take their stand for the reality of Inter-Communion in ecumenical circles.

I close with some words of Donald Baillie, the beloved schoolmate of boyhood years: "Inter-Communion should come early in the approach of the churches toward full unity in the ecumenical fellowship, for that unity can never be reached so long as the separated churches refuse to give each other the divine medicine for their healing."

✴ 8 ✴

The Church and
the World

"This is my Father's world,
    Oh let us ne'er forget,
That though the wrong seems oft so strong
    God is the ruler yet.
This is my Father's world: the battle is not done;
    Jesus who died shall be satisfied,
And earth and heaven be one."

THIS stanza is taken from a well-known hymn which was written early in the present century by a Presbyterian minister, Maltbie D. Babcock. The sentiment it expresses, regarding the sovereign and over-arching rule of God in human society and history and the certainty of Christ's victory in the world, is profoundly in accord with Reformed theology and the Presbyterian outlook. One of Calvin's famous descriptive references to the world in the divine economy calls it "The theater of God's glory." It is the place where the character of God and His eternal purpose become unveiled.

166

"THE THEATER OF GOD'S GLORY"

The world and all that is in it belongs to God. The everlasting Father and sovereign Ruler of all things is interested in everything that takes place on earth. Being no detached spectator or celestial snob, God keeps close to the life of earth, participates in its affairs, and makes the history of mankind the sphere where His inmost being is made manifest. The petition which Christ included in the Prayer He taught His disciples will be fulfilled. "Thy will be done on earth as it is done in Heaven." Inasmuch, therefore, as the victory of God is assured, all who take the living God seriously and are obedient to His will can "possess their souls in patience," while they actively engage in serving Him and their fellow men. Each can say in calm dynamic peace, like the peace of the river whose flowing waters are guided by the channel in which they move, "My times are in thy hand."

In making a place for God in the affairs of men, John Calvin did not start, as Immanuel Kant did, with a categorical imperative of Reason. He did not accept the command, "Thou shalt," and then move on by a process of inexorable logic to an affirmation that God exists. Neither did he make his starting point man's religious consciousness, or some high ethical value, supplied by culture which it is the function of religion to conserve. Calvin started from the living God who had revealed Himself historically in Jesus Christ and of whose sovereign grasp he himself had had an overwhelming experience. That God was the source of all the imperatives of the Moral Law. For that Being, who had redeemed him by his grace and claimed him for his own, he must work. And this he did, and inspired others to do the same all the days of his life, in this buoyant expectation, "The Kingdom of God is at hand."

In this same spirit, and convinced that God is working His purposes out in history, Presbyterians have approached and continue to approach their task in society. They have never been tempted to regard history as a kind of unreal show, a pageant that is being staged by a Celestial Playwright, or as an impersonal drama in which the ultimate values are not moral but aesthetic. Presbyterian thought and action have been molded by the Biblical affirmation that at the heart of history is God's unfolding purpose in Christ for the world. It is this same certainty that is enshrined in that line of Tennyson's, "Yet I doubt not through the ages one increasing purpose runs."

With this background Presbyterians have sensed the awesome contemporary significance, and felt the challenge, of the Marxist thesis of Dialectical Materialism. They affirm as much as do the Marxists that the world and everything within it must be taken seriously; for "not a sparrow falls to the ground" without God's knowledge and will. They equally affirm that historical life is not a pageant or a graveyard, but the scene of a tremendous ongoing struggle in which the victory is assured. The ultimate victory, however, shall be achieved not by the material, but by the spiritual. The group, moreover, for which the ultimate triumph is reserved is not a class called the World Proletariat, but a community composed of all classes called the Church Universal of Jesus Christ. For the same reason, however, the great ongoing struggle is one in which the tenderest concern must be shown for the poor and the disinherited throughout the world and for all the natural rights of man. Basically, however, the great struggle of our time is not the struggle between Capitalism and Communism, it is the struggle to bring to the birth a new spiritual humanity. The creation of the New Humanity in Christ is the goal of history.

Almighty God has ordained that the future shall be with the New Humanity and not with any class, or race, any nation, or culture, even should it claim to have been foreordained to victory by a dialectical principle. To make manifest the Church, the New Humanity, the People of God, to the "Principalities and Powers," that is what human life is for under God. For neither humanity as such, nor any of its manifestations, have a right to exist for themselves alone, but only for God. All life is under God and for God; and the true life of man consists in struggling with the help of God to create an order of existence which shall be of God, for God, and like God, a manifestation, as St. Paul said, of the "manifold (many colored) wisdom of God." What matters, therefore, is that life in its wholeness, whether in the Church or in society, should be adjusted to God and His eternal purpose in Christ. This is the basic Presbyterian view.

A corollary to the Lordship of God over all life is that in the world arena God is glorified in judgment as well as in mercy. He acts in judgment when the order of right relations between man and his Maker, between man and his fellow man, and between nation and nation, is deliberately violated. In Isaiah's prophetic interpretation of Israel's history the pagan power of Assyria is proclaimed to be God's instrument to punish Israel, which had become "a Godless nation." Assyria became in God's sovereign rule "the rod of my anger, the staff of my fury." Through this organ of judgment "the Lord," to use Isaiah's words, "finished all His work on Mount Zion and on Jerusalem." That accomplished, the same sovereign Lord would proceed to "punish the arrogant boasting of the King of Assyria and his haughty pride." This famous episode and its prophetic interpretation provide a perspective for the study of history in our time. Ancient Assyria could bequeath its role to some Communist nation of today which might conceivably be used by God to punish nations which cherish their heritage of faith and morals only in name, and which have forsaken the Lord God of their fathers, paying no more than lip tribute to the objectives for which their fathers lived and died. Communism would not be validated thereby as the way of the future in God's world. It could become, however, the means of revealing to some of its arrogant opponents that their way in the present courts disaster.

It is appropriate that I should quote at this point some sentences from a contemporary document entitled *A Letter to Presbyterians*, which was endorsed in May 1954 by the General Assembly of the Presbyterian Church in the U.S.A. This deliverance, which will be dealt with more fully at a later stage in our study, puts the matter thus: "Any human attempt to establish a form of world order which does no more than exalt the interests of a class, a culture, a race or a nation above God and the whole human family, is foredoomed to disaster. Ideas are on the march, forces are abroad, whose time has come. They cannot be repressed and they will bring unjust orders to an end. In the world of today all forms of feudalism, for example, are foredoomed. So, too, are all types of imperialism. Many of the revolutionary forces of our time are in great part the judgment of God upon human selfishness and complacency and upon man's forgetfulness of man. On the other hand, just because God rules in the affairs of men, Communism as a solution of the human problem is foredoomed to failure. No political order can prevail which deliberately leaves God out of account. Man has deep spiritual longings which Communism cannot satisfy. The Communistic order will eventually be shattered upon the bedrock of human nature, that is, upon the basic sins and the abysmal needs of man and society. For that reason, Communism has an approaching rendezvous with God and the moral order."

Because of their profound conviction regarding God's presence in history, Presbyterians and Presbyterian Churches have stood for a prophetic outlook upon human affairs. If the world is truly the "theater of God's glory," then human life in all its phases must be looked at and interpreted in the light of God. When a new theological journal called *Theology Today* came into being in 1944, under Presbyterian auspices, it adopted as its motto, "The Life of Man in the Light of God." It is in this light that all current ideas, attitudes and programs must be viewed, whether they be secular or religious. In the blazing radiance of the "Light of God," political expediency, power politics, nationalistic absolutism, the current conceptions of security and freedom, the prevailing purposelessness in democratic societies, the secularization of religion and the patronization of Deity, must all be examined. In this same light must the new dreams and fresh vision of emerging societies be surveyed. Amid it all, even while the darkness deepens, Christians must think and struggle in the faith that "God is the Ruler yet," and greet Tomorrow with a cheer.

CHRISTIAN VOCATION

If God is the Lord and the world is the stage where the web of human destiny is being woven "with mercy and with judgment," how should Christians play their part in the concrete setting in which their lives are spent?

To raise the question of the Christian's vocation in society is to approach an issue which, since the days of Calvin in Geneva, has been central in the thought and life of Reformed and Presbyterian churchmen. All Christians, as we emphasized earlier in this study, have been called to be "saints," to live, that is to say, as "God's men and women." When a man can say with spiritual insight, "I know who I am and what I should become," he begins to be truly alive. Deep down in the soul of every Presbyterian who can give a reason for his faith and is steeped in his theological heritage, is the conviction that, despite his personal unworthiness, he is called to be "an active human agent of the divine purpose running through the ages."

For Presbyterians the calling of the layman is as truly divine as the calling of the minister. The layman is as much called of God to work in a secular vocation as is his pastor who was ordained to become "a minister of the Word and Sacraments." The layman is quite as responsible as a minister to be a Christian in all life's relationships. It is his responsibility, so far as he is able, to use his particular position in society for the promotion of Christian truth and goodness. Art's greatest portrayal of lay vocation is the meaningful expression on the faces of those Dutch magistrates who appear in Rembrandt's great painting, "The Syndics." Each member of the group is intensely aware of his calling and is dedicated to its fulfillment. Everything they are and have they have given to God for his service. In the performance of their official duties they personalize in a secular setting what their faith has denominated the "priesthood of all believers."

How does a person discover his vocation? His spirit must be open and responsive to God. He must be sensitive, in the light of God, to the particular talents, temperament, and education which he may have, and to the significance of the doors of opportunity that God opens before him, as well as to the challenges that sound in his ears. If young men and women are utterly serious about their life calling, a quiet voice will sound in their spirit's depths, "This is the way, walk ye in it."

It is obvious that when a Christian adopts this attitude toward his vocation under God, the great standard for behavior will not be the so-called "American Way of Life," or absolute conformism to any existing pattern of life. The question will ever be, what are the timeless values of my faith? What is the mind of Christ in the situation in which I find myself? "Lord, what wilt thou have me to do?" A Christian citizen must be loyal to his country; he must assiduously fulfill his obligations as a representative of his country. But in doing so he must never cease to be Christian.

When this practice becomes the rule in Presbyterian and other Christian circles, a current trend will be reversed. An unhappy image, described as "ugly" by citizens of other countries, will be replaced by one more truly representative of our spiritual heritage, and of the values to which our churches and institutions are professedly committed. Some words spoken, in 1958, by the first General Assembly of the newly created United Presbyterian Church in the United States of America will stand repetition at this point. "Only as Church members become Christ's missionaries in their several vocations, in government and diplomacy, in industry and commerce, in the home and in the classroom, in the clinic and on the farm, will men perceive that Christ is the way, the Truth and the Life."

WORK AND WORKERS

But if a man is to fulfill his vocation in society, *work* is involved. In these days of high specialization and increasing automation, to work with one's hands or with one's mind, in some kind of production labor, is as basic and important as it was in the first century of the Christian era at the time of the Protestant Reformation, and when New England was founded by the Puritans. In each of these periods work, whether manual labor or mental toil, the conduct of government or the care of souls, was regarded as necessary activity.

John Calvin and all who were influenced by his thought and outlook laid great stress upon the indispensable necessity of work on the part of every human being, Christian and non-Christian alike. This emphasis upon work is part of the classical heritage of Presbyterians. For Presbyterians who understand and are loyal to their own spiritual tradition, society is healthy and social life is meaningful when all citizens, save those whose human situation is abnormal, are "workers" of some kind or another. Calvin's teaching on the subject of work, it has been remarked, "was in a very real sense a turning point in the history of European thought." On the one hand he maintained, as I have earlier indicated, that it was quite legitimate for a man to lend his money for interest, and that this practice could not be regarded as unscriptural, unless the amount of interest demanded were unreasonable. The inspirer of the new capitalistic order was equally clear, however, that society should have no place for social parasites who engaged in no useful endeavor. Calvin, Knox and the Founders of the American nation carried in their souls and expressed in their whole social outlook the revolutionary words of St. Paul in his Second Letter to the Thessalonians. Said the man who gloried in working with his hands to support himself and others: "When we were actually with you we gave you this principle to work on: 'If a man will not work he shall not eat.' Now we hear that you have some among you living quite undisciplined lives, never doing a stroke of work, and busy only in other people's affairs."

It is surely a paradox of history that Karl Marx, the father of Communism, picked up this principle enunciated by St. Paul and made it pivotal in his system of thought. Would to God he had become interested in other aspects of Pauline thought. If he had known, moreover, that for Calvin and Baxter "parasites and drones" had no legitimate place in God's world, and that the Puritans had no use for "idle bellies who chirp sweetly in the shade," he would not have come to the conclusion that "religion is the opiate of the people." Today a burning problem exists around the globe, especially in undeveloped countries, which Calvinistic Presbyterians and all Christians must face. It is the problem of the idle rich who live merely for pleasure, and of feudal barons, many of whom are absentee landlords, whose wide acres and princely estates are founded upon human misery.

In this connection we witness another paradox. There are men and women of wealth belonging to Presbyterian and other Christian denominations, who in the economic realm, whether they know it or not, owe their all to John Calvin who made "free enterprise" possible. It is clear, however, that were John Calvin and many a Puritan pioneer alive in our time, they would be labelled "Communists." They would be indicted by people who have accumulated wealth because of the theological outlook of Calvin and his posterity, but who, nevertheless, ignore or reject their social concern. Calvin has many heirs who cultivate charity, but who are totally unconcerned about justice. The only freedom for which they crusade is the freedom to accumulate wealth.

Christians cannot evade their social responsibility. When Presbyterians have been true to their heritage, they have flashed the white light of their faith upon every social issue. To fail to do so would be most un-Presbyterian.

CHRISTIAN RESPONSIBILITY IN THE SECULAR ORDER

For Christians and for men in general, there is something beyond making a living, supporting one's family, fulfilling one's vocation and devoting time to the chosen avocation of one's leisure. There is something far beyond being a good churchman and a citizen of personal and professional integrity.

Presbyterians, because of their theological outlook, have traditionally concerned themselves with the shape and functioning of the secular order of which their lives were a part. They have held that Christian churches, as well as individual Christians, are under obligation, so far as their influence may extend, to bring the whole life of society into harmony with the principles of God's moral government of the world. This they will strive to achieve not as sentimental romanticists or unrealistic idealists, who ignore the complexities and the dialectical paradoxes of human existence, but as people who believe that the Living God is concerned about, and involved in, the conduct of mundane affairs.

It has been the consistent position of Presbyterian churches in the Old World and the New that the Christian religion must be something very much more than the conservator of socially recognized values. A current trend, discernible in some Presbyterian circles, to use religion, the Church and Christian journalism, to buttress a specific economic or social viewpoint, runs counter to Presbyterian standards. True religion must be concerned with the moralization of life. In Calvin's matchless words, it must have as one of its objectives to "maintain humanity among men." It can never be satisfied to be merely an aspect of culture having its own sphere of action and its own privileges and rights. The Church to be truly the Church must confront culture and civilization and seek their transformation.

One of the earliest and most prophetic efforts in the history of American Christianity to face the challenge of emergent industrialism in the nineteenth century was that of a Presbyter-

ian elder, Stephen Colwell, who carried on an important man-
ufacturing business in the city of Philadelphia. This remarkable man, we are told, "divided his time between industry, religion, and political economy." In 1851, he published a book
entitled "New Themes for the Protestant Clergy." This volume
was written three years after the publication by Marx and En-
gels of *The Communist Manifesto,* and before Marx wrote *Das
Kapital.* There is no evidence that Colwell was familiar with
Marx. As a Christian, however, he was very sensitive to the
situation of work in an industrial society. "This idea," he wrote,
"of considering men as mere machines for the purpose of creating and distributing wealth, may do very well to sound off
the periods, syllogisms, and statements of political economists,
but the whole nation is totally and irreconcilably at variance
with Christianity." He sternly rebuked the Church for failing
to denounce covetousness as sin. "No violent revolution is required," he said. "What is required is that everyone who is,
or who believes himself to be, a true disciple of Christ should
at once resolve, so far as he might be favored with divine aid,
to live in this world according to the teachings of his Master."

James Dombrowski, who published in 1936 a book entitled
"The Early Days of Christian Socialism in America," a volume
issued by the Columbia University Press, makes these significant remarks about Stephen Colwell and his ideas. "Colwell
was not a socialist and preferred the method of Christian
'charity'—a term which he used in the sense of brotherliness,
not as mere almsgiving. Yet he saw in Socialism's demand for
social justice, and in its criticism of Capitalism, a position
which had much in common with Christianity, Colwell saw
in the vague stirring of revolt among the workers of the world
a natural and desirable reaction against injustice. He cau-
tioned 'stern Christian conservatives' not to denounce them.
The lack of faith in so-called infidels often might be traced,
he said, to a passion for the welfare of humanity which had
been outraged by the failure of organized religion to lend as-
sistance to their work of reform. He named Paine as an example. 'They find Christians arrayed against their plans, and

they immediately array themselves against Christianity.'"
How very true this has been historically; how true it also is today!

Colwell's concern that the American clergy should be made
sensitively aware of the great new issue which was beginning
to confront society and the Church, founded a Chair of Christian Ethics in Princeton Theological Seminary, of which he
was himself a Trustee. This was the first Chair of Christian
Ethics to be established in any Seminary in America and the
world.

In the present century Presbyterian concern for the industrial worker has shown itself in a number of ways. At the beginning of the present century there was organized by the
Presbyterian Church the Workingman's Department, which
afterwards became the Department of Church and Labor.
Presbyterians were among the first to manifest this kind of
social concern. As concrete institutional expression of this concern they founded Labor Temple, a new type of church, in one
of the most congested areas of New York City. Labor Temple
was designed to be in every respect a real workingman's
Church, which workingmen themselves would run. In a few
years the initiative became famous the world over. (*Presbyterian Enterprise*, Armstrong, Loetscher, Anderson, pp. 270-
276.)

In 1910, at the close of the decade which saw Labor Temple
and the new *Federal Council of the Churches of Christ in
America* come into being, the General Assembly of the Presbyterian Church made a number of social pronouncements.
At the head of these was the following affirmation: "The
Church declares that the getting of wealth must be in obedience to Christian ideals, and that all wealth, from whatever
source acquired, must be held or administered as a trust from
God for the good of fellowmen. The Church emphasizes the
danger, ever imminent to the individual and to society as well,
of setting material welfare above righteous life. The Church
protests against undue desire for wealth, untempered pursuit
of gain, and the immoderate exaltation of riches." These

words are particularly relevant today, half a century after they were uttered, when material prosperity is regarded as the chief sign of divine favor.

Outstanding in recent decades has been Presbyterian concern for Industrial Evangelism in the United States and abroad. The Presbyterian Church has gone squarely on record through its General Assembly as favoring voluntary abstinence from alcoholic beverages, and it promotes an interest in the restoration of alcoholics. The Church's Committee on Social Education and Action has, ever since its founding in 1936, given outstanding leadership in informing the mind and sensitizing the conscience of Presbyterians on the great social issues of our time. The Committee has become in a very real sense the Church's social conscience. Its annual report to the General Assembly is always the occasion for one of the most exciting and creative sessions of that body.

While the Presbyterian Church does not deal officially with the problem of farm labor, save insofar as spiritual help is provided for migrant workers, Presbyterians have played a leading part in creating and developing the National Advisory Committee on Farm Labor. The soul of this initiative, which is designed to deal with the most shocking single situation in the social life of America, the hapless condition of nearly three million migrant farm laborers, the great majority of whom are American-born, is an elder of the Southern Presbyterian Church, Dr. Frank P. Graham. Dr. Graham, former United States Senator, and for many years President of the University of North Carolina, is now the United Nations Mediator between India and Pakistan. He represents in his person the incarnation of Presbyterianism at its best in relation to the social welfare of human beings.

On the subject of race relations which constitutes the most acute social issue in contemporary American life, both the United Presbyterian Church U.S.A. and its sister denomination, the Presbyterian Church U.S., have gone on record, through their respective General Assemblies, as being in favor of promoting a non-segregation policy throughout their constituency. There are, it is true, Presbyterian groups, institutions, and even Presbyteries, which oppose a policy of full civil rights and social equality for negroes. But every effort toward a Christian solution of this complex historic problem has the blessing of Presbyterian leaders in both Churches and the sanction of their supreme judicatories. Negroes are now elected Moderators of leading Presbyteries and figure in high administrative positions in Church Boards and Commissions. In many instances, white ministers are co-pastors with negro colleagues in integrated congregations. The General Assembly of the United Presbyterian Church will meet in no city where negro commissioners cannot enjoy the same hotel facilities as their white brethren, and on a basis of complete equality. So, "though the wrong seems oft so strong, God is the Ruler yet." The "Presbyterian Way" is not yet the "Christian Way," but an increasing number of pilgrims who take seriously their Lord's injunction to be "the light of the world" are on the march towards the sunrise.

THE STATE, THE CHURCH, AND RELIGIOUS FREEDOM

It is the historic faith of Presbyterians that the Christian Church is the "Foundation of the World." This doctrine was proclaimed by Calvin, who was inspired by Paul's mystic rapture regarding the Church in his Ephesian Letter. Presbyterians have also held with Calvin and the great Apostle that the "State was ordained by God."

A high view of the state has always marked Presbyterian thought and outlook. While rejecting as blasphemous the Hegelian thesis that the state is "God walking on earth," a view which was foundational in Nazi thought and is native to Fascism, Presbyterians have regarded the state, when it is concerned about morality and justice, as God's agent in establishing and maintaining order in the world. In Calvin's thought, rulers are to be viewed as "God's subordinate executives." In virtue of their office they are "gods" under God, in the sense in which the term is used in a passage quoted by Jesus in the

Fourth Gospel: "I said, you are gods." For the great Genevan the state exists ultimately for the sake of the Church, it being necessary for the Church's well-being. The secular power, when it pursues its true objectives under God, secures the right to worship. It also secures order and promotes the exercise of the human virtues. But as God is the source of all government there can be no legitimate exercise of power that is not based on morality and justice.

In his view of the state, therefore, Calvin stands at a dynamic point in the center of a triangle each of whose three sides represents an alien view. The state is no mere man-made authority; it owes its status to no "social contract" into which men voluntarily enter, as was maintained by Rousseau. The state is not a divinity in its own right, as Hegel and Hitler proclaimed. Neither is the state merely a supreme principle of order which has no inherent right to introduce and enforce legislation regarded as being in the best interests of citizens as a whole, but whose enforcement would curtail some cherished advantages traditionally enjoyed by a small minority. This is a view held by some Presbyterian men of wealth. There is no doubt however that for Calvin, Knox and the New England Puritans the welfare of all the people was a primary function of the state. In the truest, purest sense of the term, those men envisaged a "welfare state" under God, in which the state would be God's servant for the good of people. For Calvin the state as God's servant was a creation of God, but of God's Common Grace, whereas the Church was created by His Special Grace. Nevertheless, the state, that is the government as such, is sacred and holy. It is as necessary to mankind as "heat and water, light and air." The theocratic idea of the state is thus basic in Calvin's thinking. God is over the people, but the people have authority over rulers under God.

But now comes the great divide in Presbyterian history in the matter of Church-State relations. Both Calvin and Knox and the authors of the *Westminster Confession of Faith* believed in the "establishment principle," that is, in the establishment of the Church or a church, as the Church of the nation. The state would give the Church certain privileges, support and authority. The Church, on its part, would acknowledge the right of the state to intervene in certain circumstances in Church affairs, in order to guarantee that the Church continued loyal to obligations which it had solemnly contracted. This position, American Presbyterians have rejected. From the time immediately following the War of Independence, when the first General Assembly of the Presbyterian Church in America was constituted, the Church has consistently advocated complete separation between Church and State. In 1788 the old chapter on "The Civil Magistrate" was rewritten in the terms cited earlier in this book. From that time Presbyterians have been in the forefront of those who have opposed both the intervention of the State in the spiritual affairs of the Church, and the acceptance by any Church of special favors and privileges from the State.

While this is the "Presbyterian Way," as it is also the "American Way," certain things need to be clearly emphasized, even at the expense of reiteration.

Under all ordinary circumstances any kind of government, by the fact that it has a status in its own right under God, is to be obeyed for conscience's sake. The attitude toward religion of those in authority is indifferent where civil obedience is concerned. The Presbyterian Constitution lays down that "infidelity, or difference in religion, doth not make void the magistrate's just and legal authority, nor free the people from their due obedience to him, from which ecclesiastical persons are not exempted."

The authority of government is to be challenged by citizens only when it would compel them to do things which they believe to be contrary to the will of God. Inasmuch as "God alone is Lord of the conscience," He is to be obeyed above all earthly rulers, whatever be the cost of obedience. This principle is equally applicable whether the government concerned has been democratically elected, or whether it be an authoritarian form of government which has come into power not by the will of the people, but by force.

At the present time there are churches in certain European countries, Spain, Czechoslovakia and Hungary, for example, which are obliged to accept the social and political situation in which they find themselves, simply because there is nothing they can do about it. Their condition is analogous to that of the Church in the Rome of Nero. Among those churches are important members of the World Presbyterian Alliance. They accommodate themselves as best they can to their situation. They do not enjoy full religious freedom such as fellow Presbyterians in the United States enjoy. But they do have freedom to engage in public worship and to preach the Gospel. In their theological seminaries, moreover, they have freedom to criticize Marxism and the Communist view of life. In Hungary and Czechoslovakia the present Communist regime continues the traditional practice of previous governments, and gives state aid to all the Churches, both Roman Catholic and Protestant. In much the same way, as is still customary in England and Sweden, the government has the last word as to who shall be elected to Episcopal leadership in the churches which enjoy state patronage. Unless they are forced to profess theological ideas which run counter to their Christian faith, and to engage in practices which violate their conscience, Christian churches in Communist lands can do no more than put their trust in God and wait patiently for a better day.

THE CHURCH CHALLENGES THE STATE

On the other hand, when Christians in such countries find themselves in a situation where they have to make a choice between denying the absolute Lordship of Jesus Christ over all life, or accepting the Marxist philosophy of life, they have no recourse but to follow their Lord and take the consequence of their loyalty. This was the kind of situation created in Germany in the time of the Nazis. Hitler went far beyond what the Communists have ever attempted to do. He set out to oblige the Churches in Germany to accept the Nazi ideology regarding the Messianic role of the German Führer, with its view of the German nation as the new "People of God," the race of destiny. To have accepted this demand would have made the churches mere instruments of state policy. It was then that, under the leadership of men of the Reformed tradition, in particular, Karl Barth and Wilhelm Niessel, the famous Declaration of Barmen was issued in 1934. This historic document proclaimed the unique and solitary Lordship of Jesus Christ over the Church and Nation and all things human. Karl Barth, being a Swiss citizen, was obliged to return to his country. Niessel, the "Iron Niessel," as he was called, went to prison. In the post-Nazi era this deeply spiritual man and profound theological thinker has played a leading part in the work of the World Presbyterian Alliance.

Happily, the American nation and the churches within its boundaries have never been subjected to a situation in which a dictatorship of any kind has held sway. In the fifties of the present century, however, a phenomenon appeared of an essentially Fascist nature which, for several years, constituted a serious threat to freedom of thought and association in both Church and society. Founded upon the assumption that the supreme absolute for behavior in our time was to be Anti-Communist, and holding that ethical and religious attitudes, as well as human relationships, were to be judged by the measure in which they opposed Communism, or, on the other hand, appeared to favor causes in which Communists too might be interested, this phenomenon became the cause of untold misery and injustice in the lives of thousands of American citizens. It destroyed moral perspective, dulled human sensitivity, introduced a false notion of the meaning of security, restored the spirit and methods of the Spanish Inquisition, and brought great discredit upon the United States among the nations of the world.

The phenomenon in question became associated with the name of a United States Senator called McCarthy, who emerged as the incarnation and driving force of a new un-American, inhuman, and anti-Christian crusade. The Senator in question obtained very considerable backing both in Congress and in the Executive branch of government. He also had the support of many men of wealth, for whom the supreme freedom was untrammelled liberty to make money, while freedom's greatest enemy was the pretension to curb that freedom in the interests of society as a whole. Even churchmen, especially men for whom religion was primarily a social relationship, or perchance an inner force that gave one power to achieve success, supported what became known as McCarthyism, and which at this writing is by no means dead.

It was when Senator McCarthy was at the peak of his power and thousands of the nation's most loyal citizens in government posts, in university chairs, in positions of Church leadership, were becoming suspect of having Communist sympathies that the General Council of the Presbyterian Church U.S.A. issued a communication to all its ministers and congregations throughout the nation. The document was entitled, "A Letter to Presbyterians concerning the Present Situation in Our Country and in the World." It was dated October 21, 1953 and was signed by the Chairman and Secretary of the Council. The "Letter" was a reasoned and potent attack upon the menace which confronted the nation, and, at the same time, upon the assumptions and mood which made this menace possible. Its thought was inspired by the Bible and by truths which have inspired Presbyterian thought and life through the centuries.

From the day when the full text of "A Letter to Presbyterians," some 2,700 words in length, was printed by the *New York Times*, the national and world press gave it unusual publicity. According to European opinion no religious document in the history of American Christianity ever received so much attention in the secular press of Europe. *Le Monde* of Paris reprinted it in full in two successive issues. The annual gatherings of sister denominations in the United States took up the strain during the remainder of 1953 and throughout 1954. On the eve of the Presbyterian General Assembly in May, 1954, a leading weekly magazine, with a circulation of several millions, printed a reactionary feature article. The thesis of this article was that "A Letter to Presbyterians" was based upon two successive numbers of the Communist Cominform Journal, which the authors of the "Letter" had never seen! But the Assembly of nearly a thousand members was not to be intimidated. The communication of its General Council was enthusiastically endorsed. Notice was thereby served upon the new Inquisition that the Churches of the nation and the American people in general would not tolerate for long its sinister procedures. Shortly thereafter, Associate-Justice Douglass, of the Supreme Court, published a book which he called *Almanac of Liberty*. The day, October 21, he said, will be linked in the history of the American Republic with "A Letter to Presbyterians."

What was it that the "Letter" said? Here are some of the sentiments to which it gave expression: "A subtle but potent assault upon basic human rights is now in progress. Treason and dissent are being confused. The shrine of conscience and private judgment, which God alone has a right to enter, is being invaded. Un-American attitudes towards ideas and books are becoming current. Attacks are being made upon citizens of integrity and social passion which are utterly alien to our democratic tradition. . . . A great many people, within and without our government, approach the problem of Communism in a purely negative way. Communism, which is at bottom a secular religious faith of great vitality, is thus being dealt with as an exclusively police problem. Totally devoid of a constructive program of action, this negativism is in danger of leading the American mind into a spiritual vacuum. Our national house, cleansed of one demon, would invite by its very emptiness the entrance of seven others. In the case of a national crisis this emptiness could, in the high sounding name of security, be occupied with ease by a Fascist tyranny."

Citing a pronouncement made by the General Assembly of 1953 to the effect that "it is a basic emphasis in our Presbyterian heritage of faith that all human life should be lived in accordance with the principles established by God for the life of men and nations," the "Letter" proceeded thus: "We suggest, therefore, that all Presbyterians give earnest consideration to the following three basic principles and their implications for our thought and life."

"One: The Christian Church has a prophetic mission to fulfill in every society and in every age."

"Two: The majesty of Truth must be preserved at all times and at all costs."

"Three: God's sovereign rule is the controlling factor in history."

Affirming that "Ideas are on the march, forces are abroad, whose time has come and which will bring unjust orders to an end;" emphasizing the fact that "wherever a religion, a political system or a social order does not interest itself in the common people, violent revolt eventually takes place;" proclaiming that "Communism as a solution of the human problem is foredoomed to failure and that the Communistic order will eventually be shattered upon the bedrock of human nature," a plea is made that "Communists, Communist nations and Communist-ruled peoples should be our concern." A dynamic, personal approach to the whole problem of Communism is urged. "In hating a system let us not allow ourselves to hate individuals or whole nations," says the "Letter." "History and experience teach us that persons and peoples do change. Let us ever be on the lookout for the evidence of change in the Communist world, for the effects of disillusionment, and for the presence of a God-implanted hunger. Such disillusionment and hunger can be met only by a sympathetic approach and a disposition to listen and confer."

Then follows a passionate appeal for face-to-face encounter with Communist enemies at the highest level. "Let us always be ready to meet around a conference table with the rulers of Communist countries. . . . In human conflicts there is no substitute for negotiation. Direct personal conference has been God's way with man from the beginning. 'Come now and let us reason together' was the Word of God to Israel through the

Prophet Isaiah. We must take the risk and even the initiative, of seeking face-to-face encounter with our enemies."

It is a happy coincidence that in the intervening years since "A Letter to Presbyterians" was issued, the principle of personal encounter and negotiation at the highest level between the representatives of enemy nations has begun to be taken seriously. In the meantime we witness also a recrudescence of the most banal form of vilification. The attempt has been made to inspire in government circles, and even among the Armed Services, a suspicion of churchmen, churches and the National Council of churches. But inexorable Laws of God's moral order will take care of all "who delight in lies" and "bear false witness."

In the meantime, the "Presbyterian Way," and the way of all who take seriously their holy Christian Faith, is to "rejoice in the Lord and wait patiently for Him," remembering the while,

> "That though the wrong seems oft so strong,
>   God is the Ruler yet."

A Global Family of Faith

P<small>ART</small> of the debt we owe to that strange German philosopher, Count Hermann Keyserling, is the importance he always assigned to "representative data." I will try to be loyal
to this principle in descanting on World Presbyterianism.

It will be thrilling, in the not distant future, for Presbyterians and others to have authoritative studies made available
of the more than fourscore autonomous Church bodies bearing the name of Presbyterian or Reformed which are scattered
throughout the globe. My task is much less ambitious. It is to
deal with what is most representative in World Presbyterianism at the present time, as regards significant developments,
attitudes and relationships.

THE WORLD PRESBYTERIAN ALLIANCE

I begin with the body which constitutes the organizational
link between the great majority of Presbyterians and Reformed Christians around the globe. "The World Presbyterian
Alliance," or more properly "The Alliance of Reformed
Churches around the World Holding the Presbyterian Order," held its first meeting in Edinburgh, the Scottish capital,
in 1877. Two years before that date representatives of
churches in the Reformed tradition from Great Britain and

Continental Europe met with representatives from sister churches in the United States and Canada to organize the "Alliance" and draft a constitution. This meeting was historic. For the first time since the Reformation of the sixteenth century, a group of autonomous Protestant churches belonging to the same Confessional family came together to establish an organizational bond between them.

The Constitution of the new organization was prefaced by a Preamble. This Preamble is so significant, because of the light it sheds upon the spirit of those who created the Presbyterian Alliance, that I quote it in its entirety. It is the kind of "representative" deliverance which breathes and interprets the inmost soul of Presbyterianism.

"*Whereas,* Churches holding the Reformed faith and organized on Presbyterian principles are found, though under a variety of names, in different parts of the world:

"*Whereas,* many of these were long wont to maintain close relations, but are at present united by no visible bond, whether of fellowship or of work: and

"*Whereas,* in the providence of God the time seems to have come when they may all more fully manifest their essential oneness, have closer communion with each other, and promote great causes by joint action:

"It is agreed to form a Presbyterian Alliance to meet in General Council from time to time in order to confer on matters of common interest, and to further the ends for which the Church has been constituted by her divine Lord and only King.

"In forming this Alliance the Presbyterian Churches do not mean to change their fraternal relations with other Churches, but will be ready as heretofore, to join with them in Christian fellowship, and in advancing the cause of the Redeemer, on the general principle maintained and taught in the Reformed Confessions that the Church on earth, though composed of many members, is One Body, in the Communion of the Holy Ghost, of which Body Christ is the Supreme Head, and the Scriptures alone are the infallible law."

Here are struck some of the classical notes in the Reformed heritage of faith and life. A "visible bond" for "fellowship" and "work" should unite Churches that belong to a common Christian tradition. Whatever they do together should be directed toward "furthering the ends" for which the Church was constituted by "her divine Lord and only King." The one Church of God on earth of which Presbyterian Churches are a part must never cease to be the supreme object of loyalty. The question as to how the "cause of the Redeemer" can best be advanced through the Church can be answered only by the Bible.

Regarding membership in the Alliance, the Constitution of the new body laid down as follows: "Any Church organized on Presbyterian principles which holds the supreme authority of the Scriptures of the Old and New Testaments in matters of faith and morals, and whose creed is in harmony with the consensus of the Reformed Confessions, shall be eligible for admission into the Alliance." Here is a ground for membership which is at once basic and broad. It has never been the genius of Presbyterianism to give foundational status to points of theological interpretation, provided the great essentials of the faith are unqualifiedly accepted.

At intervals of three or more years, depending on world conditions, the General Council of the Alliance met in different countries of Europe and North America. When the Council met in Princeton, New Jersey, in 1954, there lay behind it a record of sixteen previous gatherings. Meetings had been held in Scotland, England, Ireland, Wales, Switzerland, Canada and the United States. In the meantime eight other Protestant Confessions had established World organizations, Anglicans, Methodists, Baptists, Lutherans, Congregationalists, Disciples of Christ, Pentecostals and the Society of Friends.

For eighty years the organization of the World Presbyterian Alliance was exceedingly simple. The only full-time officer was a General Secretary. Through a quarterly which he edited, the General Secretary kept the member Churches of the Alliance informed regarding important happenings in the several constituent communions, and supplied them with articles and news items of common interest or concern. Between meetings of the Council an Executive Commission divided into two sections, an Eastern and a Western, promoted "the objects of the Alliance" and made arrangements for the next world gathering. No fund existed for publicity or promotion, or to provide support for member churches in special need.

The Councils and Sections of the Alliance, when they convened, were always memorable occasions for those attending. The fellowship was rich; important addresses were delivered on themes relating to Presbyterian doctrine and witness; receptions were given to the representatives of the churches by local bodies; the delegates and guests carried away inspiring memories of great utterances and of friendships old and new. The proceedings of each Council were published in an impressive volume. But nothing happened. It is true, of course, that it never was the purpose of the Alliance to legislate for the member churches, far less to carry on administrative activities in their name and for their sake. Apart from individual addresses of a very high order and significance, little was done corporately to probe into the inner depths of the Reformed tradition and to explore the contribution it should be making, in the light and strength of the Holy Spirit, to the human situation. It was the glory, however, of the World Presbyterian Alliance during all those years to eschew any vestige of a sectarian spirit or ambition. It was Christian and not Presbyterian truth that was proclaimed as should be done in every time and clime and circumstance.

What was still lacking was a reflective awareness of Presbyterianism's role in the total spiritual situation. I can recall a meeting of Presbyterian and Reformed delegates to the Second Faith and Order Conference which met in Edinburgh in 1937. We were summoned together by Principal Curtis of New College, who had been President of the Alliance from 1933 to 1937. His words made a profound impression upon all who heard him. "Among the Protestant Confessions," he said, "we Presbyterians have done least to define our doctrine of the Church. This puts us at a great disadvantage when we engage in discussion with other Christian churchmen."

Several significant things happened during the early decades of the twentieth century. The concept of the Church Universal, and the awareness of its concrete emergence around the world, summoned Presbyterian and other Protestant Christians to dedicate themselves to a united Christian approach to all spiritual issues. In those decades the Ecumenical Movement was born and was accorded the benediction and hearty support of Presbyterians. In some countries, it is true, particularly in Scotland, leading Presbyterians, with a few notable exceptions, conscientiously felt that there was no real place for the World Presbyterian Alliance or for World Confessionalism of any kind! It was maintained that in view of the organization of the World Council of Churches the pursuit of Confessional unity could not be justified. The recognized leaders of some Presbyterian churches showed slight interest in the Alliance.

The case of Scotland was quite unique. In the early years of the century a generation emerged which had practically ceased to think of Scottish Presbyterianism as belonging to an historic and existent world-wide confessional family. The Church of Scotland, once again united in the twenties, tended to think of itself as a National Church, that is, as the Church of the Scottish nation, part of whose mission was to project itself throughout the British Commonwealth and wherever Scottish people were found. It is both interesting and significant in this connection that, historically speaking, the term "Presbyterian" had never appeared in the official title of either the Church of Scotland or of the United Free Church of Scotland, the churches which became reunited in 1929. In the meantime a tension arose between the churches established by the Colonial Committee and the new churches established in the mission fields of the world by the historic Committee on Foreign Missions.

In the Scotland of today, however, a generation has arisen

which is dedicated to restoring Scottish Presbyterianism to a sense of its Reformed heritage. Its members are ecumenically minded. They are devoted to the pursuit of Christian unity and are dedicated to the fulfillment of the Christian's world mission. At the same time they are unreservedly committed to the proposition that a virile and creative ecumenism needs the insights which the Holy Spirit communicated to Presbyterian and Reformed churches in the course of their experience and witness through the centuries. For that reason the celebration in October, 1960, of the Four Hundredth Anniversary of the Scottish Reformation under John Knox can be epoch-making in the religious life of Scotland, as well as in the witness of the world-wide Presbyterian family.

PRINCETON 1954

The meeting of the Seventeenth General Council of the Alliance at Princeton in August 1954 gave Presbyterians a new sense of mission, and the work of the Alliance a fresh start. The new spirit and concerns which had become manifest at the meeting of the Sixteenth General Council in Geneva, Switzerland in 1948, soon after the close of the Second World War, and on the eve of the founding of the World Council of Churches in Amsterdam, Holland, made themselves felt. For the first time in its history the Alliance met in a small community. It was a community, however, which was saturated with Presbyterian and American history. Its location, moreover, was midway between two vast cities, New York and Philadelphia, which modest Princetonians speak of as their two large "suburbs"!

During the days of the Council's meeting in the home community of John Witherspoon and Charles Hodge, of James McCosh and Woodrow Wilson, and where Albert Einstein had established his dwelling, things took place which were of very great significance for the development of the "Alliance of Reformed Churches Throughout the World Holding the Presbyterian Order."

The main theme chosen for the sessions of the Council was "The Witness of the Reformed Churches in the World Today." It was made unmistakably clear that the spirit of the gathering was not sectarian. At the very first session, the speaker charged with opening up the Main Theme referred to a declaration drafted by the Executive Committee of the Alliance at a meeting in Basel, Switzerland, in 1951. With the words, *"We are not, and we should never become, an ecclesiastical power bloc,"* he went on to quote from the Basel Declaration. Two of the sentences are particularly relevant. "The supreme purpose of the Alliance is not to promote World Presbyterianism as an end in itself, but to make the Reformed tradition the servant of God's redemptive purpose through the wider agency of the Church Universal. In the judgment of the Committee we are charged by God to see to it that the resurgence of denominationalism, which is manifest around the globe, shall now become sectarian but shall remain ecumenical in character." The Council subsequently made the entire Basel Declaration its own. It sought to crystallize at the same time the elements of unique emphasis in the Reformed heritage to which witness should be borne within the fellowship of the Church Universal. Other sentiments contained in the Basel statement will be referred to in the next chapter, when we come to deal specifically with the relationship of Presbyterianism to the world-wide family of faith.

Profoundly sensitive to changed conditions in the total world situation, as well as among Reformed Churches throughout the world, the Council proceeded to take a number of important actions. Modifications were introduced into the Constitution of the Alliance to meet the new situation. Significant and typical were two articles relating to Church union and to religious and civil liberty. The new Constitution affirmed:

"It shall be the purpose of the Alliance to study what unions and reunions of the constituent churches of the Alliance, with each other or with other churches, appear to be according to the Will of God, to make recommendations growing out of such study and to give such help as may be desirable."

It shall also be the purpose of the Alliance:

"To promote and defend religious and civil liberty whenever threatened throughout the world."

Provision was made in the Constitution for the organization of new areas of the Alliance beyond the traditional "Eastern and Western Sections." This was done in view of the greatly expanded boundaries within which member Churches were located. Provision was also made for "Permanent departments, commissions and committees" of the Alliance to be established from time to time, when authorized by the General Council or the Executive Committee. This provision opened the way for important developments which took place in the organization of the Alliance during the interval between the Princeton gathering and the Eighteenth Meeting of the Alliance in São Paulo, Brazil.

Before passing on to describe and appraise the epoch-making gathering of Presbyterian and Reformed Christians, which took place in the Republic of Brazil in 1959, let me close this section by citing some paragraphs from the Message to the Constituent Churches which was sent down to them from Princeton. How relevant these words continue to be:

"Many in our time, in all lands, are filled with fear for their economic security, the stability of their institutions, the future of their nations, fear of a war which will destroy the basis of our civilization, fear sometimes of life itself, or of death as if it were the final evil.

"And to many of our contemporaries Christ seems to offer no hope. We confess that at our best the light in our churches is so pale a reflection of Him Who is the Light of the World, and the life in our churches lacks so much of the Savour of His preserving salt, that multitudes have to look elsewhere for their understanding of life, their duty, and their assurance.

"Under these circumstances the sharpest challenge to us who have certain faith in the Crucified, Risen and Victorious Christ is so to live and teach that faith that men may see in Christ the only real hope for mankind, the one effectual remedy for all their fears, and so to witness that no one shall be turned away from the Christian hope by our default. For any hope but that which is in Him will finally succumb before life's limitations and tragedies, or break on the rock of God's eternal justice.

"We beg you, therefore, to heed God's Living Word as it comes to you through the Scriptures.

Claim the whole world for Jesus Christ,
Seek to close the divided Christian ranks.
Love all men, even your enemies, knowing that they too are called to become children in God's family.
Strive to break down racial barriers, to promote understanding between classes and peoples, to provide an opportunity for every man to enjoy his share of God's bounty and to earn a livelihood for himself and his family."

SÃO PAULO 1959

When the Eighteenth General Council of the World Presbyterian Alliance met in the Brazilian city of São Paulo on July 27, 1959, a precedent which had lasted for eight decades was broken, and the Alliance entered upon a new phase of its history.

Hitherto Council meetings had invariably been held in Europe or North America. Now the largest and most representative Council in the long series convened on Brazil's central plateau, in the most populous and progressive city of the Republic. In this vast industrial metropolis of more than three million inhabitants, celebrated for decades as the fastest growing city in the world, three hundred delegates of Presbyterian and reformed churches met together for a period of ten days. They had come from seventy-eight churches in fifty-three nations and represented a total constituency of forty-six million members. They found themselves in a land which is territorially the vastest in the Western Hemisphere. It is a country, moreover, where the most complete religious liberty prevails and in which the Protestant population of three millions is growing at a phenomenal rate. And to the honor of the Brazilian Republic let this too be said! No land on earth is so free from racial prejudice as is Brazil. Here the sons of daughters of Europeans, Asians, Africans, and Brazil's own aboriginal inhabitants live together in peace.

The hall of meeting was quite unique. It was a circular dome-shaped structure in which, some years before, a great exhibition was held in honor of the four hundredth anniversary of the founding of São Paulo. In this historical pavilion of many rooms, their walls adorned with products of Brazilian art and with scenes from the country's past, the sessions of the Council were held. From the great open spaces of the park in which the historical pavilion is situated could be seen the fantastic silhouette of São Paulo's towering skyscrapers with their daring and original architectural designs. On their way each morning to the place of meeting the delegates could gaze at hovels of human misery situated side by side with monuments of material grandeur. The sight was a daily parable of the traditional chasm which exists between the rich and the poor in this beloved country, as in so many other countries of the world.

Amid the symbols of Brazil's past and present, and not far distant from scenes of glory and of shame, were held the sessions of the first Protestant church body ever to hold a world assembly in Latin-American territory. It was a fascinating and inspiring thought that the Council now meeting was itself of Latin origin, its founder being a Frenchman called John Calvin. It was this same Calvin, moreover, who had sent to Brazil in the sixteenth century the first Protestant mission ever to arrive in the country.

From time to time as the work of the Council proceeded, fraternal delegates from other Confessional bodies were introduced and given an opportunity to speak. These special guests ran the Protestant ecclesiastical gamut, from Anglicans to Pentecostals. It was the first time that a representative of the world-wide Pentecostal movement was officially welcomed in a world gathering sponsored by one of the historic Christian traditions.

Morning by morning at eight a.m. the Council was led in

Bible study by two representatives of the Hispanic world. One represented the daughter lands in the Americas, the other the Iberian Peninsula, the great mother of the Spanish and Portuguese speaking peoples. Rev. Boanerges Ribeiro, a young Brazilian pastor, a man of vision and growing power, led us on the mornings of the first week; a veteran Spaniard, Dr. Manuel Gutierrez Marin, the doughty incarnation of Spanish Protestantism, led our meditations on the second.

The concentrated thought of the Council was devoted in both plenary sessions and sectional groups to the Council's Main Theme: "The Servant Lord and His Servant People." It was impressive to sense how the "servant" image had stirred the imagination and quickened the intellect of all who were present. It became more and more clear, through Biblical exposition and theological discourse, that the image of the "servant" is the symbol which is most native to the Bible and to the Christian religion, whether to describe a true man in relation to his Father in Heaven, or the Eternal Son of God Who, for man's salvation, took the "form of a servant."

It became evident also as the discussion proceeded, that this image, which symbolizes the instrumental character of everything human and finite in relation to Deity, is an emphasis which lies at the heart of the Reformed tradition and witness. This fact became abundantly plain as the several facets of the Theme were opened up. Theology and man, the Church and the State, it was pointed out, will all serve the ends for which they exist, and so fulfill their true destiny, when they are servants of God. It became equally apparent that no image in the Christian religion is more relevant to the needs of mankind today, whether in the realm of thought or of action, than "the form of a servant." No image, moreover, stands in more desperate need of being restored to its pristine Biblical significance. Let me repeat what I have written in the Introduction to the Council's Proceedings. "Today when the Christian Church and secular institutions tend to glory in what they have or in what they are, it is imperative that all people be made to see that neither they nor their creations can have any true future in God's world unless they be willing one and all to 'take the form of a servant.' "

The great newspapers of São Paulo and Rio de Janeiro, and they are among the world's greatest, gave an unusual amount of space to the unique theme of the Council, as well as to its personalities and the proceedings in general. One thing grew upon Latin American Presbyterians and upon all who had knowledge of the religious situation in the Hispanic world as a whole. It was this. The greatest single need of this vast area of the globe, where religion has been so largely repudiated, is that people should come to realize that Jesus Christ and the Christian Church have a unique service to render to life and culture and to the general welfare of mankind.

After business sessions had considered the concrete needs of the Alliance and made provision to meet them, the Council's Message to the Churches was presented and approved. I quote its very significant central paragraph: "Human life is 'the theater of God's glory,' and He has called us each one to His great service as we find our true life in Jesus Christ who has inaugurated the New Humanity. To be fully human and to enjoy fulness of life, we have to be linked to God's great purpose in Jesus Christ the Servant Lord. When men no longer have to be convinced about whether life makes sense, but only about what sense life makes, they are set free from self-righteousness, cynicism and despair. They acquire instead an authentic allegiance and a steadfast purpose. They are given the freedom of His service."

I conclude this section with a reference to the great public gathering with which the São Paulo Council came to a close. In the large cathedral-like sanctuary belonging to the Independent Presbyterian Church of Brazil, the Council delegates, surrounded by several thousand Brazilian Presbyterians, celebrated the Sacrament of the Lord's Supper. Before the Communion Service, which was conducted by the new President of the Alliance, the retiring President hung around the neck of his successor, a symbolic jewel. This jewel, made of gold and enamel, had been passed from one Alliance president to another, ever since the Belfast meeting in 1934. A glance at its symbolism provides an appropriate closing for this account of the São Paulo meeting. On the front side of the jewel these words appear in letters of gold, "General Presbyterian Alliance: Calvin-Knox-Zwingli-1875," forming a circle around the historic emblem of the Burning Bush, the bush that "burned and was not consumed." On the reverse side, enclosing a seven-branched golden candlestick, are inscribed the Latin words "Lampades Multae Una Lux," "Many lamps, One Light."

These emblems from the Old Testament and the New became strangely alive as one viewed from the pulpit the representatives of World Presbyterianism seated in the central nave of the great church. Men and women were there from churches under active persecution, or whose religious freedom was very severely circumscribed by the State, brethren from Spain and Colombia, from Hungary and Czechoslovakia. Mingled with them, many in the costumes of their native country, were Chinese and Koreans, Indians and Singhalese, Indonesians and Filipinos, citizens of Ghana and Nigeria, Egypt and the Union of South Africa. They partook together of the symbols of Christ's broken body and shed blood alongside fellow Christians of the Reformed tradition who hailed from Churches in Continental Europe, Great Britain, North America and the far reaches of the English speaking world. They were all of them loyal to the heritage of Calvin, Knox and Zwingli. Yet with fellow Christians everywhere, and in the spirit of those men, they gave their supreme allegiance to the one Lord Jesus Christ, the Head of the Church, and to the one Church, which is His Body, and which continues to burn but is not consumed.

The day following this closing session, the great majority of the delegates drove from the uplands to the sea along one of the world's most picturesque highways. Their destination was Rio de Janeiro, where they would attend the celebration of the First Centennial of the National Presbyterian Church of Brazil. This memorable event will now engage our attention.

THE FIRST CENTENNIAL OF PRESBYTERIANISM IN BRAZIL

In the early weeks of the present year a Brazilian friend sent me an unusual memento of the unforgetable week spent in Rio following the São Paulo gathering. It was nothing less than a postage stamp which the Brazilian Government had just issued to commemorate a celebration which I and many fellow Presbyterians had been privileged to attend. Bordering the historic symbol of the Burning Bush were the words, "First Century of Presbyterian Work in Brazil."

Looking at this stamp, a stranger to Brazil and to the Brazilian tradition might think that some kind of Church-State relationship existed in this country, or at least that the Republic was the sponsor of religious activity. The opposite is true. The Brazilian nation, whose motto is "Order and Progress" is ever ready to recognize, without prejudice, whatever appears to make a creative contribution to the national life. Some years previously the government had issued a similar stamp in honor of an international Congress of Baptist Youth.

So far as Presbyterianism in Brazil is concerned, the authorities had a rich variety of objective evidence upon which to base their appraisal and inspire their symbolic appreciation of the "Presbyterian way" in the nation's history. In the capital itself, there is a downtown avenue which bears the name of Erasmo Braga. Braga was a great Presbyterian churchman, scholar, and saint who consecrated his life to the cause of Christian unity. He passed away in the thirties of the present century. In the same city there is a public square called after an eminent Presbyterian pastor, Alvaro Reis, who had labored for several decades in a nearby church. In São Paulo there is a great educational institution called Mackenzie University. Founded and basically administered by Presbyterians, although for the past half century, it has had no direct Church connections, Mackenzie with its seven thousand students is the largest and most diversified center of learning ever founded by Americans in any part of the world. Many of Brazil's leading architects and engineers were educated in its halls. In the neighboring state of Minas Geraes, and located in the city of Lavras, is a famous School of Agriculture, called Gammon Institute, which was founded and is supported by the Southern Presbyterian Church in the United States. One of its recent presidents, Benjamin Hunnicutt, who later became President of Mackenzie, was decorated by the Government of Brazil.

In addition to these institutions, Presbyterian churches and missions in Brazil have founded and carry on a large number of schools, hospitals, orphanages and welfare agencies from the Atlantic Coast to the Amazonian forests. Presbyterians have figured, moreover, among the country's poets, men of letters and grammarians. In a representative Presbyterian congregation in Brazil today, the membership runs the gamut from manual workers through clerks, businessmen and teachers, to persons occupying important positions in government service and leading posts in the armed forces.

It was in recognition of facts of this kind that the Brazilian Government was led to issue the special stamp to which reference has been made. It was for the same reason that two other events happened in which the Republic of Brazil sought to honor the Presbyterian contribution to the nation's life.

On the twelfth of August, 1959, the day that the Centennial celebration came to an end, several members of the National Congress rose in their places in the Chamber of Deputies. They delivered stirring addresses in eulogy of the many ways in which Presbyterians, national and foreign, had made the country their debtors. These very detailed and eloquent tributes were printed in the Congressional Record.

The same evening an event occurred which is without precedent in the political history of the Hispanic World. The closing session of the Centennial festivities in the Presbyterian Cathedral of Rio was attended by the President of the Brazilian Republic. Never before had the head of a Latin American state made an official appearance in a Protestant place of worship to speak on behalf of his government. The singing and prayer over, President Kubitschek arose and delivered an address. Speaking, he said, as a Christian and a member of the Roman Catholic Church, he rejoiced in the complete religious freedom prevailing in the Brazilian nation. He desired to express the appreciation of the government and people of Brazil for all that Presbyterians and other Protestant Christians had meant in the life and culture of the country. He then retired to fulfill another engagement and the meeting continued. But history had been made. The presence of the President of Brazil in a Protestant place of worship was the symbol of a new status for Evangelical Christianity in the Continent South of Panama.

But what Brazilian Presbyterians themselves are most grateful for today is the direct influence of the Gospel in their lives and in the life of their nation. They had gathered together from the remotest frontiers of the country to commemorate the arrival in Brazil one hundred years ago of the first Presbyterian missionary from the United States, a young man named Ashbel Green Simonton. On Sunday, the eighth of August, the commemoration services began and were designed to continue in one form or another for a whole year. The spirit of the anniversary occasion was made concrete in a special motto which was blazoned in flags and emblems and printed on manifold folders, magazines and books, "A Year of Gratitude for a Century of Blessing" (*Um ano de gratidão por um século de bênção*). This gratitude was for the harvest which had begun to appear in soil where the seed of the Gospel has been sown across the years. This was the keynote struck in the Centennial hymn which called upon the Presbyterians of today to live worthily of the "struggles, sacrifices and prayers" of those who had gone before.

It was my own ninth visit to Brazil. The first was in 1926 when a friend dearly beloved, Erasmo Braga, to whom I owed an unspeakable debt of gratitude, was still alive. On this occasion it was my privilege to preach the opening sermon of the "Year of Gratitude" in the Cathedral Church of Rio, where I had spoken on many previous occasions. I had seen the Presbyterian Church grow across the years and its witness deepen and expand.

REFLECTION FROM A MISSIONARY FRONTIER

I conclude this chapter by sharing some reflections regarding the "Presbyterian Way" in Brazil. Brazilian Presbyterians are representative products of the missionary zeal which has brought into being other "Younger Churches" in different parts of the world.

It is a fact of history, all too frequently forgotten, that the Reformed tradition is of Latin origin. It was French fellow countrymen of John Calvin who were the first Protestant missionaries to set foot on Latin American soil. This was in the middle of the sixteenth century. In 1551, soon after Brazil was discovered, the first Protestant sermon ever preached in the Western Hemisphere was delivered by the Calvinist minister, Pierre Richier. Richier was the pioneer of a movement to establish in America "a refuge for the persecuted faithful in France, Spain, and any other part" and to carry the Gospel to the West. Due to the treachery of one-time friends in the Government of France, the movement, after a couple of decades, came to a tragic end, leaving behind a tale of martyrdom.

Three whole centuries passed before another representative of the Calvinist tradition appeared in Brazil. Ashbel Green Simonton, a Pennsylvanian, born in the region of the old Log College, and a graduate of Princeton Theological Seminary, landed in Rio de Janeiro in 1859 as the first Presbyterian missionary from the United States. He founded the First Presbyterian Church of Rio. After a brief but dedicated and fruitful career, Simonton died of yellow fever in the city of São Paulo in 1867.

In the interval between Simonton's death and the celebration of his arrival in the country, Presbyterian missions and Brazilian born converts to the Gospel brought into being a Presbyterian family of 250,000 communicant members. In recent years a great westward movement has taken place. In many instances the erection of a Presbyterian place of worship coincided with the founding of a new city, so that the Church became the center of community life. The progress of Presbyterianism in Brazil has been marked by great evangelistic fervor, which, however, has never interfered with the diversified form in which the spirit of Christ and the Presbyterian passion to meet human need found expression.

In the course of the past hundred years, several important events took place in the development of Brazilian Presbyterianism. Some were tragic, some creative. Both may be regarded as representative of the "Presbyterian way" in Brazil and elsewhere throughout the world. Nothing has been further from my mind in writing this book than to appear to glorify Presbyterianism as the perfect, far less, the only "way." Presbyterians have had their failures, as all Christians and Christian Churches have had and continue to have. Nothing is to be lost, but everything to be gained, by frank self-examination in the light of Him who alone is the perfect "Way."

In 1903 the Presbyterian Church in Brazil was rent by a schism. As has so frequently happened in Christian history, the main cause of division was not a profound issue relating to the inner structure of the faith. The Church became divided on the question as to whether it was proper that members of secret societies such as the Masonic Order, for example, should be admitted to full membership in the Christian Church. There were other causes as well, personality conflicts and tensions between missionaries and nationals. In fact, the Masonic issue was really a scapegoat for deeper cleavages. Those who refused to admit Masons to membership in the Church formed the Independent Presbyterian Church of Brazil, severing relations with missionaries and the mother Church in the U.S.A. The main segment of the Church, however, kept on its way maintaining all its former relationships, while continuing to exercise complete autonomy as an independent self-supporting Church.

For half a century each segment of the Church produced illustrious figures and achieved notable results. But, as a consequence of this schism, not only the Presbyterian cause suffered in Brazil, but also the whole Evangelical witness in the country. How thrilling it was, therefore, that the Centennial celebration became the occasion for an official commitment on the part of both Churches to seek reunion. They both participated in closest comradeship in commemorating their common origin. On the eve of the great Anniversary their respective Moderators, each a most distinguished figure in his own right, joined together in issuing a remarkable document which may well prove historic in the development of Brazilian Protestantism. In this *Manifesto,* dated August 1959, José Borges dos Santos, Jr. and Seth Ferraz, after dealing extensively with what Brazilian Presbyterianism has stood for and accomplished, proceed to define their common task. From some luminous and moving paragraphs I cull the following:

"Our principal task is to proclaim the Gospel and promote the application of the teaching of Jesus. . . .

"But the Church's task as we seek to fulfill it is in no sense sectarian. It is not reasonable to work, struggle and suffer merely to make Protestants or Presbyterians. There is only one task which is really worthy of us all; to make disciples of Jesus Christ.

"We are not the Gospel. We announce the Gospel.

"Sectarianism is the poison of the spiritual life. In a land where the dangers that threaten youth are multiplying in an alarming manner, there is no way except that of fraternal collaboration in every possible manner, between the various branches of the Christian Church. Theological hate is one of the factors responsible for producing a climate favorable to atheism and unbelief.

"Brazil's great need is Christ in the hearts of men and of men in the midst of the world.

"Christ taught that the unmistakable mark of His disciples was in no sense aggressiveness, fanaticism or intolerance. What distinguishes the followers of Christ is affectionate and human comprehension. It is of them that the words speak 'By this will all men know that you are my disciples if you love one another.' "

In this "Manifesto," which I trust will soon be reproduced in English in its entirety, we find a background which is symbolical of all Presbyterian history. There is always a shining beam and a deep, dark shadow. The beam is a consistent, unsectarian, commitment to Christ's Lordship in the soul, in the Church and in the world, and to the one Church which is Christ's Body. This beam has shone brightly from Calvin's time to the present. But its light has been shadowed many a time during the past four centuries, and in every continent of the world, by a fanatical intolerance of legitimate differences of viewpoint. This shadow has often denied the faith, divided the Church, and stained Presbyterian annals. It eclipsed for a moment the radiant figure and witness of John Calvin himself when he gave his consent to the death of Servetus. It has since then obscured Presbyterian witness through schism or unworthy controversy, or by the presence on the Presbyterian road through history of groups for whom loyalty to Christ consists in discovering stains in the witness of Christian brethren.

This paradox, dialectic, dichotomy, contradiction—call it what you will—has appeared historically in Scotland and the United States, in Brazil, Ceylon, and most recently in Korea. But in the end, in the spirit of the Brazilian "Manifesto," and of the glorious healing of a recent short-lived schism in Korea, the gleam from Him Who is the Everlasting Way pierces the shadow on the "Presbyterian way." It is natural, I suppose, that a religious tradition, which has stressed the reality of original sin, should be able out of its own annals to provide illustrations of the same!

With this reflection on a "representative" phenomenon let us pass on. The presence in Brazil for the historic gatherings in São Paulo and Rio de Janeiro of many representatives from the sister Presbyterian churches in the United States, which had once been one, had also far-reaching significance. A prolonged conference between delegates of the Brazilian Church, American missionaries to Brazil, and members of the recently constituted Commission on Ecumenical Mission and Relations of the United Presbyterian Church in the U.S.A., dealt not only with Church-mission relationships, but with issues that concern the whole missionary movement in the Ecumenical Era. It was the "representative" character of this three-way encounter that leads me to refer to it as I conclude this chapter.

It became evident that a famous formulation of Christian strategy called the "Brazil Plan," which was founded on the idea that in a vast country like Brazil, missions and the National Church should carry on their work with a certain degree of independence of one another, was no longer possible or desirable. Measures were taken to secure a more dynamic relationship in terms of an overall strategy which would embrace the National Church, the "Sending Churches" and their missions. A Mission, which has had a glorious record of creative Christian endeavor, both in institutions of all kinds and on the lonely frontiers of pioneer Evangelism, will henceforth become more closely related to the National Presbyterian Church if not actually integrated into its structure. The National Church representatives, on their part, shared with missionaries and Commission members their dream of a new theological seminary in the interior of the country which would supplement the work of its great Seminary in Campinas. They outlined the steps that had been taken to establish a Presbyterian Church in the heart of Brasilia, the nation's new capital, and shared the growing vision of missionary endeavor in the Amazonian wilds. For all of these projects the closest cooperation is needed.

Through this encounter American Presbyterians were supplied with abundant evidence of the rightness of the decision which had changed the name and character of the old Boards of Foreign Missions into a body more representative of the Church, and more adjusted to the realities of the Christian World Mission today. This body bears the significant name "The Commission on Ecumenical Mission and Relations." Interpreting the term "ecumenical" as both the fulfillment of the Church's mission, and the pursuit of the Church's unity, in obedience to the mandate of Jesus Christ that His followers be one that the world may believe, the new Commission has adopted as its watchword "Into all the World Together."

✠ 10 ✠

Presbyterians and
the Church Universal

C HIEF among the words that have become current in Christian circles, during the last quarter of a century, is the word "ecumenical." It has become common to speak of the "Ecumenical Movement," whether or not it be regarded as "the great new fact of our time." It is derived from the Greek word "oikoumene," which means "the inhabited earth."

In secular, as well as in religious settings, men use the term "ecumenical." They speak for example of the "ecumenical era." By that they mean that all thinking must be done in the awareness that, as a result of technological advance the "oikoumene" has, for better or for worse, become one in a way never before true in human history. Today political revolution or a chemical explosion can be so violent, can have such far-reaching consequences, and be given such world-wide publicity, that the times have become "ecumenical." Mankind is bound together in unprecedented human solidarity. This is true, whatever tomorrow may have in store of sorrow or of joy for the human kind, whether it be tragic co-extinction, or friendly co-existence.

This is the contemporary context, the fateful shadow, in

which we consider the attitude of Presbyterians toward fellow Christians in the "Ecumenical Era." But let me hasten to add, while a powerful case can be made for the promotion of world-wide Christian solidarity upon the grounds of expediency, this is not the true ground upon which to advocate the realization of Christian oneness around the globe. Nor is the advocacy of such an ecumenical motive necessary. What is needed is that Christians everywhere should realize that they belong by nature to a universal fellowship, and that, whatever be the special urgency of the times, they should become what they already are, a single family in Christ. The members of the One Church, which is the Body of Christ, are under obligation to have fellowship with one another as they have fellowship with Him Who is their Head.

Not only are Presbyterians committed by their doctrinal standards to affirm and promote the unity of the One Church, they have also throughout their history occupied a vanguard position in working for Christian solidarity and in giving concrete, visible expression to the Church Universal.

THE HOLY CATHOLIC CHURCH AND THE COMMUNION OF SAINTS

John Calvin, who is freely regarded as the most ecumenical figure in the Reformation era, would heartily endorse the dictum attributed to the early Church Father, Ignatius of Antioch, "Where Christ is, there is the Church." Both Calvin and his fellow Reformers in the sixteenth century never thought for a moment that they were creating a new Church. The goal of their reforming efforts was to bring the existing Church under the judgment of the Word of God in order to restore it to its pristine form, spirit and witness. For Calvin the true Church was to be found "wherever we find the Word of God purely preached and heard and the Sacraments administered according to the institution of Christ." He emphasized, moreover, the obligation of all Christians "to cultivate the communion of the Universal Visible Church." "As there is but one Head of the faithful," said he, "so they ought all to be united in One Body; thus there are not several Churches, but only one which is extended throughout all the world."

In the true spirit of Calvin, the Westminster Confession of Faith conceives the Visible Church, the Church Militant, in these terms: It too is "Catholic or Universal under the Gospel." It "consists of all those throughout the world that profess the true religion together with their children, and is the Kingdom of the Lord Jesus Christ, the house and family of God." The Westminster Divines recognized, however, that in every visible manifestation of the Church there will be imperfections. No absolute purity can be looked for. They say, therefore, "This Catholic Church has been sometimes more, sometimes less visible. And particular Churches, which are members thereof, are more or less pure, according as the doctrine of the Gospel is taught and embraced, ordinances administered, and public worship performed more or less purely in them." Then comes this solemn recognition: "The purest Churches under heaven are subject both to mixture and error."

Recognizing in all humility that no Christian Church can fully meet Christ's standards, and that individual Christians can never fully measure up to the high ideal of Christian sainthood, all who bear the name of Christ and profess to be "Christ's men and women," are under solemn obligation to maintain friendly relations with one another in the unity of the faith. Presbyterians read in their Confession of Faith these words: "Saints by profession are bound to maintain a holy fellowship and communion in the worship of God, and in performing such other spiritual services as tend to their mutual edification; as also in relieving each other in outward things, according to their several abilities and necessities." Then comes the ecumenical injunction, which is sacredly enshrined in Presbyterian doctrine and is native to the genius of the Reformed faith: "*Which communion* (in worship and mutual helpfulness), *as God offereth opportunity, is to be extended unto all those who in every place call upon the name of the Lord Jesus.*" Could there be a more decisive testimony to what it means, in a practical sense, to belong to the Holy Catholic Church or a more articulate clarion call to intercommunion?

But let it not be thought that all Presbyterians have taken seriously this classical commitment to the Church Universal or even the injunction to cultivate the Communion of Saints. The main stream of Presbyterian witness has been shadowed by a type of sectarian Presbyterianism which, as was suggested in the last chapter, has been schismatic, sometimes even glorying in schism as the clearest evidence of loyalty to Christ. The slogan, "Come out from among them and be ye separate," has resounded at many times and in many places in the course of Presbyterian history. Sometimes it has been heard in a non-Christian environment, sometimes in a traditional stronghold of the great Roman communion, sometimes in a country whose national history is steeped in Presbyterian tradition. The Son of God, who enjoined His followers to love one another, has often "been crucified afresh and put to an open shame." I can recall an unusual instance in which during the celebration of the Lord's Supper, and while the communicants were seated at the Table, an elder who was distributing the elements, received instructions from the presiding minister to bypass a man who was known to belong to another Church. All the others received the bread and wine, but this Christian stranger was excluded from "the Communion of Saints."

I mention the above case for several reasons. In the first place, this most unseemly behavior in the name of superior orthodoxy and close communion, runs counter to Presbyterian doctrine and practice. Open communion for strangers who are members of a Christian Church, and who desire to enjoy the "communion of Saints" by joining in the Holy Communion with Presbyterian fellow Christians, is a privilege granted by every major Presbyterian church around the world. In the second place, the refusal to admit to "the Communion of Saints," through participation in the Sacrament of the Lord's Supper, fellow Christians belonging to denominations not regarded as "Christian" in the full sense, is not limited to sectarian Presbyterians. The practice of "closed communion" is found today among many types of "gathered churches"; but it is universal among those communions to whom the designation "High Churchism" may be applied.

Presbyterians, let it be emphasized, have a high view of the Church and of the significance of the Eucharistic feast. They consider, however, that the "Communion of Saints" can never be real, and that the reality of the Holy Catholic Church is denied, wherever those who have professed their faith in Christ and live "holy in Christ Jesus" are denied access to the Table called by His name and where He is the Unseen Host. For Presbyterians the free participation of Christians in this "Holy Ordinance instituted by Christ" should be regarded as the true starting point and not the consummation of ecumenical unity.

It was in this spirit that the Seventeenth General Council of the World Presbyterian Alliance at its meeting at Princeton in 1956 said as follows:

"As Reformed and Presbyterian Churches, we bear witness to our fellow Christians that we recognize the ministry, Sacraments and membership of all Churches which, according to the Bible, confess Jesus Christ as Lord and Savior. We invite and gladly welcome the members of all such churches to the Table of our Common Lord. The Church has received the Sacrament of the Holy Communion from Christ and He communicates Himself in it to the believer. The Table of the Lord is His not ours. We believe that we dare not refuse the Sacrament to any baptized person who loves and confesses Jesus Christ as Lord and Savior. It is our conviction that unwillingness, particularly at this time, to practice such intercommunion gravely impedes the cause of unity and lends an air of unreality to much of our talk about it. We cannot proclaim the Gospel of reconciliation without demonstrating at the Table of the Lord that we are reconciled to one another. Therefore, we would welcome face-to-face talks with fellow Christians in other Churches looking forward to the time when all sincere Christians will be welcome around a Common Table."

Presbyterian dedication to the cause of Christian unity and cooperative effort is founded in theological conviction regarding the nature of the Church. It has expressed itself historically in a great variety of ways.

Calvin's idea of a free and universal council, and his plea that Christians should regard one another with "judgments of charity," has lived on down the centuries. The ecumenical current flowed steadily onwards, though its course was marked from time to time by a cataract roar of fanaticism or intolerance. Commitment to the essentials of the "faith once for all committed to the Saints," and loyalty to the "Presbyterian way" in the government of the Church, were combined with a rich human concern for intercommunion with other Christians. In the seventeenth century, those sons of Calvin, Comenius, the Czech, and Baxter, the Englishman, were ardent advocates of Christian unity.

It was not, however, until the nineteenth century that the ecumenical tide began to rise. In Scotland in the middle of the century, and in the United States simultaneously, through the presence in the country of the great Scottish missionary to India, Alexander Duff, a concern for Christian unity was awakened. Duff's visit to America became the occasion for the first *Union Missionary Convention*. It was held in New York City in 1854. "Its object," according to the Report, "was to unite in cordial love and sympathy the friends of missions."

Nearly fifty years passed before another great interdenominational gathering of the friends of missions assembled in the United States. When it did convene in 1900 in New York City, it turned out to be the largest interdenominational Christian gathering ever held, whether before or since. It bore, moreover, the significant title, *"The Ecumenical Missionary Con-*

ference." Two things of great significance are to be noted regarding this gathering. According to the Report of the Conference, the connecting link between this New York meeting and the first world-wide missionary conference in history, which was held in London in 1888, was "the Fifth General Council of the Alliance of the Reformed Churches holding the Presbyterian System, held in Toronto, Canada, September 21-30, 1892." The proposal was made at this Alliance meeting that such a conference should be held, and Presbyterians played a leading part in carrying out the proposal.

The second thing worthy of note is that for the first time in more than a thousand years the word "ecumenical" appeared in the title of a Christian gathering. What is even more significant is that in the title of the New York gathering this term is not used as expressive of the pursuit of world-wide unity. The term is employed in its more basic meaning of the fulfillment of world-wide mission. "This Conference is called 'ecumenical,'" said one of the organizers of the meeting, "not because all portions of the Christian Church are to be represented in it by delegates, but because the plan of campaign which it proposes covers the whole area of the inhabited globe." It was united missionary commitment and vision that inspired the Conference and bestowed upon it the dynamic designation "ecumenical." But the movement toward Christian unity as an ecclesiastical or theological concern had not yet dawned. The "Ecumenical Conference" of 1900 broke up without a council, or even so much as a committee, being set up to continue its work.

The organizers of the epoch-making *World Missionary Conference*, which convened in Edinburgh in 1910, found it inexpedient for ecclesiastical reasons to use the term "ecumenical" in designating the gathering. The result was that the word passed into disuse in Protestant Church circles until it was resuscitated in 1937 at the Oxford Conference on "Church, Community and State." In the Roman Catholic Church, "ecumenical" had by this time no more than an historical significance. It suggested merely the seven Councils of the Undivided Church.

God forgive any semblance of Confessional pride, or any undue emphasis upon Presbyterian commitment to Christian unity and the contribution of individual Presbyterians to the ecumenical cause. History's annals, however, enshrine certain facts which reveal in how many instances Presbyterians were used by God to promote the unity and mission of His Church during the present century. He was pleased to use the Commission of the Oxford Conference on "The Universal Church and the World of Nations," which was presided over by a Presbyterian chairman, to clarify the concept of "ecumenical." The Commission's Report set in high relief the basic difference between the "ecumenical" problem and the "international" problem. It also pleased God to use Presbyterian leadership at the 1951 meeting of the Central Committee of the World Council of Churches in Rolle, Switzerland, to secure that "ecumenical" should not be used exclusively to connote the Church's pursuit of unity around the world, but should equally connote the fulfillment of its God-given mission throughout the world. The Rolle conception, which still stands unchallenged is in these terms: "It is important to insist that this word (ecumenical), which comes from the Greek word for the whole inhabited earth is properly used to describe *everything that relates to the whole task of the whole Church to bring the Gospel to the whole world.* It therefore covers equally the missionary movement and the movement towards unity and must not be used to describe the latter in contradiction to the former."

Some years later, in God's sovereign providence, a Presbyterian impulse in Lucknow, India, led to the reconstruction of the Joint Committee of the World Council of Churches and the International Missionary Council. The Presbyterian Chairman of the Committee, sensing the overwhelming desire of the representatives of the Younger Churches, that a common approach should be made to the unity of the Church and the mission of the Church, initiated the process which has been underway for several years to integrate the two ecumenical bodies. Under the leadership of a new chairman of the Joint Committee, also a Presbyterian, the General Assembly of the World Council of Churches, due to meet in New Delhi, India, in 1961, will be asked to approve the integration of the two Councils, a proposal to which the International Missionary Council, the chairman of which is an African Presbyterian minister, who is a citizen of the new Republic of Ghana, is already committed.

In the past few decades two very outstanding and symbolic Church unions have taken place in Asia and the Western World, both of which have crossed traditional ecclesiastical boundaries. One brought into being the Church of South India, the other, the United Church of Canada. Presbyterians took the lead in promoting the former. The first Moderator of the United Church of Canada in which Congregationalists, Methodists and Presbyterians are joined together was Dr. George Pidgeon, the beloved pastor of Bloor Street Presbyterian Church, Toronto.

Considering the zeal with which Reformed and Presbyterian churches have sought to serve the Church Universal, it is not surprising that a Dutch Calvinist, a minister of the Reformed Church of Holland, has been the General Secretary of the World Council of Churches since the organization of the Council in 1948. It is more also than mere coincidence that a Presbyterian should be the World Council's chief representative in the United States, and that his predecessor, another Presbyterian, was the first General Secretary of the National Council of the Churches of Christ in America.

On the missionary side of the Ecumenical movement it was an initiative taken by the Board of Foreign Missions of the Presbyterian Church U.S.A. that led to the organization a few years ago of the East Asia Christian Conference. This great autonomous, regional body is the first of its kind in Christian history. Functioning within the unity of the World Council of Churches, it represents an endeavor on the part of many national churches in many Asian lands, in close partnership with the representatives of missionary societies, to advance the World Mission of the Christian Church. The Presbyterian missionary society, whose vision gave the impulse that led eventually to the creation of the East Asia Christian Conference, has since blazed a new trail. It has become transformed, as indicated in the previous chapter, into *The Commission on Ecumenical Mission and Relations*. Enshrined in this name is the conviction of a leading Presbyterian denomination that henceforth the missionary task of the Church of Christ must be carried on in all the world in close and confiding partnership between the so-called "older" and "younger" churches. These must go "Into all the World Together."

The vision involved in these developments finds an institutional interpretation in a new chair founded two decades ago in a Presbyterian theological seminary. In 1938, the year after the Oxford Conference, there was created in Princeton Seminary the Chair of Ecumenics. Two things were new, the name of the chair, and the ground it was designed to cover. The term "Ecumenics" was specially minted as the most appropriate designation to connote a field of study which would embrace both the mission of the Church and the unity of the Church. "Ecumenics" was defined as "The Science of the Church Universal, conceived as a world missionary community, its nature, its mission, its relations and its strategy." The conception of "missions" was expanded to embrace the essential task or mission of the whole Church and of all the churches. The Church exists to be missionary and cannot be regarded as being truly the Church if it is not missionary. For to be missionary belongs to the very essence of the Church. And for the Church to fulfill its total mission means that it should exercise a *prophetic* function, a *redemptive* function and a *unitive* function.

Thus the Church of Christ, not as an object of retrospective gaze for purposes of historical research, but as the subject of an ongoing life that creates history, was given a new status in theological education. Only when every phase of seminary

training, Biblical, historical, theological and practical con-
tributes to a luminous understanding of the Church Universal
and engenders a dynamic commitment to its God-given mission, can the Christian Church fulfill its destiny. Then and only
then will talk about the "ecumenical" being escape the peril of
becoming mere ecclesiastical jargon.

CONCERNING RESURGENT CONFESSIONALISM

But now we confront a paradox. At the very time
that Presbyterians and other Church leaders are devotedly
promoting the Ecumenical Movement they are, with no less
devotion, developing the world-wide solidarity of the Confessions to which they belong. In doing so, are they insincere, are
they illogical, are they irresponsible? By no means. These two
enthusiasms are not incompatible.

The truth is this. There is no future to a vague, colorless,
lowest common denominator, ecumenism. You cannot belong
to the Christian Church in general, any more than you can belong to the human race in general. "The merely cosmopolitan
is characterless," it has been well said; "Mankind as such has
no face." A distinguished professor of Princeton University,
Dr. Horton Davies, has written a book entitled "The Worship
of the English Puritans." His aim, as he indicates, is to make
a contribution to ecumenical understanding and unity. This
he seeks to do by making available to other Christians the
cherished heirloom in the realm of worship which belongs to
the Reformed tradition to which Baptists and Congregationalists, as well as Presbyterians belong. These words are significant: "The reunion of the Christian churches," says Professor
Davies, "cannot come to fruition on the sand of expediency
nor on the clay of sentimentalism. Its seed is sown on the soil
of souls that is both receptive in its understanding of our deep
spiritual unity in Christ, and also firm enough to refuse to
give up what is most precious in our own traditions." Then he
goes on to quote the words of Karl Barth, "Unity cannot come

in a crepuscular setting, which blurs distinctions, where all
cats are grey."

What is taking place in the confessional resurgence which
marks this ecumenical era is not a return to "ecclesiastical
tribalism." It is true that in certain contingencies Confessionalism could wreck the Ecumenical Movement. But the ecumenical spirit and context of the Confessional Movement is such
that a tragic outcome of this kind is exceedingly remote. Confessional leaders are committed to the Church Universal and
to the supreme Lordship of Christ. They are also sensitive to
the beckoning of the Holy Spirit and to the ominous signs of
the times by which God speaks. They are far from being like
those people about whom Thomas Carlyle once wrote in anger, who were "deaf to God's voice, blind to all but parch-
ments, and antiquarian rubrics when the divine handwriting is
abroad on the sky."

THE GLORY AND PERIL OF THE LOCAL

The next creative step in the development of true Christian
ecumenicity, by which the Church Universal becomes a World
Missionary Community, is to rediscover and transfigure the
local. It is at the local level that we find the everlastingly
human. As Presbyterians see it, one of the perils that beset
Ecumenism at the present time is that of becoming detached
from the place where the mass of Christian people live and
think and worship and serve. Between the stratospheric realm
of the ecumenical and the work-a-day world of the local, there
is a great gulf fixed.

Yet it is at the local level, where people actually live, that
the great encounters take place, that the most vital decisions
are made, that the most transforming changes are produced.
Unless Christians, in the concrete situation in which they
"live, move and have their being," come to appreciate the
significance of the Ecumenical Movement, the movement can
have no real future. And the only way in which the Ecumeni-

cal can become relevant to the Local is through the Confessional bodies to which local congregations belong. People must be reborn; they must be inspired with the riches of their own heritage of faith, if they are to tread with vision and enthusiasm the Ecumenical Way. Presbyterians must experience the reality of Christ through an exploration of their own heritage if they are to bring understanding and zeal to the cause of Christ's Church Universal.

There is an old Spanish proverb which says, "A bird may fly to the ends of the earth, but only in a nest can it raise a family." This is as true of the eagle as it is of the sparrow. What takes place in a nest, in bare crag or leafy bow, may be slow and monotonous, and totally alien to all that is spectacular and dramatic. But the process of birth and growth cannot be hastened; it must be inexorably obeyed.

On the other hand, there is always the danger that the local may become parochial. It can so easily shut itself off from the outside world, showing hostility to every influence that might threaten the proud purity of its own way of life. As Presbyterians well know, this is precisely what has happened to some members of their own confessional family. Glorying in their purity, they have stuck fast where Calvin left them; while their other brethren, in Calvin's spirit, moved forward on the Road.

Let me illumine this Presbyterian phenomenon by a parable. In a rugged mountain region of Old Castile there is a dwarfed people. Its men and women are low of stature and have suffered from rickets and other ailments that stunt human development. Some students of the situation have held that the arrested growth of this mountain folk was due to lack of sunshine in their deep ravines; others have believed that tainted water was to blame. The Spanish writer, Unamuno, however, to whom I owe the tale, and who himself visited the region, held a different view. In Unamuno's judgment the dwarflike stature of those people was due not to tainted water but to water that was excessively pure! The unhappy denizens of those uplands drank water which never had a chance of picking up salts from the earth, especially iodine, that indispensable ingredient, in all health-giving water. Unamuno turned his tale into a parable thus: "The person who tries to live by pure categories becomes a stunted dwarf." And just this, alas, has been the fate of many a Christian group among the communions and sects of the Church Universal.

While this is tragically true, the great Confessions hold the key to the future of the Ecumenical Movement. Nothing whatever is gained by the kind of ecumenical bigotry which disdains and censures any manifestation of confessional enthusiasm or loyalty. Those who look down their "ecumenical" noses at Christian brethren who, while believing that the Holy Spirit brought into being the Confession to which they belong, nevertheless, subject their tradition to constant scrutiny in the light of the Bible, Christ and their sister traditions, betray an ignorance of the ways of God and man.

One of the fruits of a genuine confessional movement that maintains itself open to the guidance of the Holy Spirit as He illumines Holy Scripture, that remains sensitive to contemporary need, that is concerned to promote the unity and mission of the Church Universal, will be the emergence of a truly ecumenical theology. What would be the marks of such a theology? Let me repeat what I wrote a number of years ago and feel more deeply today even than I did then: The theological statement to which the Church Universal should look forward must be no doctrinal syncretism or theological dilution. It must have at the heart of it no pale, lowest common denominator formula. Never must the Church sponsor a blanched, eviscerated, spineless statement of its faith. It must give birth in this revolutionary transition time to a full-blooded, loyally Biblical, unashamedly ecumenical, and strongly vertebrate system of Christian belief.

THE END OF THE WAY

I have said more than once in the course of this study that it is of the essence of Presbyterian doctrine that the unity and mission of the Church Universal must be the cherished concern of all who bear the Presbyterian name. But theological reflection is not the only basis upon which to ground adhesion to the ecumenical cause.

Let me revert once again to the lyrical and take up the strain which inspired the prologue to "The Presbyterian Way of Life." My commitment to the Holy Catholic Church and its world mission is the fruit of something much more profound and personal than a mere doctrinal imperative, or even than the example of a host of admired figures from John Calvin to Karl Barth. My Presbyterian soul has loved and worked for the Church Universal of my divine Lord and Saviour Jesus Christ, not merely because of a conviction that this is what every Christian should do. The supreme impulse to tread the Ecumenical Way has been the unspeakable debt I owe to other Church families, and to Christians living and dead, who loved my Lord but rendered Him service as members of traditions different from my own. I also know that in saying this I speak for a multitude of Presbyterians besides myself.

With this rhapsody I come to the end of "The Presbyterian Way."

About the Author

The Rev. John A. Mackay is known as one of the world's outstanding Presbyterian clergymen, and as a distinguished leader of the Ecumenical movement. Dr. Mackay has written many books, including: *Christianity on the Frontier, God's Order,* and *Preface to Christian Theology, The Other Spanish Christ,* and was editor of "Theology Today" for seven years. Born in Scotland and educated at the University of Aberdeen, he studied at the Princeton Theological Seminary and later in Spain. From 1926 to 1932 he served as lecturer and writer under the South American Federation of YMCA. In 1936 he became professor of Ecumenics and President of the Princeton Theological Seminary, where he presided until his retirement in 1959.

Index

A

Aberdeen University, 56, 131
Aberdeen University Press, 66
Abraham, 64
Abram, 160
absolutistic confessionalism, vi
Alaska, 25
alcoholic beverages, voluntary abstinence from, 178
Alexander, Archibald, 25
Allan, Tom, 157
Alliance of "Eastern and Western Sections," 195
"Alliance of Reformed Churches Throughout the World Holding the Presbyterian Order," 193
Almanac of Liberty, 185
American Board of Foreign Missions, 12
see also Presbyterian Church
American Revolution, the, 22
"American Way of Life," 172, 181
Amsterdam, Holland, 193

Anglicans, 190, 197
Annual Assembly, 138
Apostles' Creed, 53, 65, 155
Aquinas, Thomas, 10, 39, 43
Apocalypse, 10
Ascent of Mount Carmel, iv
Assembly of Divines, 45
Assemblies, 138
"Associate Reformed Presbyterian Church," 26
Assyria, as God's instrument, 169
"Auburn Affirmation, The," 51
Australian Presbyterian Church, The, 5

B

Babcock, Maltbie D., 167
Babylon, waters of, ii
Bach, 38
Baillie, Dr. Donald, 162, 165
Baptism,
    definition of, 159
    immersion as a means of, 159
    of an adult, 158
    significance of, 158

227